CW01086098

Hunting Grizzlys, Black Bear and Lions "Big-Time" on the Old Ranches

Will F. Evans
Author

Hunting Grizzlys, Black Bear and Lions
"Big-Time"
on the Old Ranches

by

WILL F. EVANS

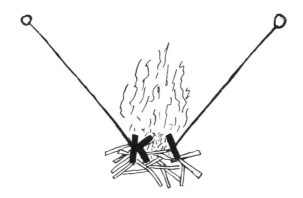

Other Books by Will Evans:

Border Skylines

Printed by

THE MCMATH CO., INC.

El Paso, Texas

1950

This Edition by

HIGH-LONESOME BOOKS

Silver City, New Mexico

2001

ISBN #0-944383-55-6

Cover photo, circa 1905: the Evans family on a bear hunt at "The Rock-pile".
George Evans is pictured at center, with beard.

Dedicated to the memory of the pioneers
who settled the Davis Mountains
in the early Eighties

Hunting Grizzlys, Black Bear and Lions
"Big-Time"
on the Old Ranches

By WILL F. EVANS

AUTHOR OF BORDER SKYLINES

FOREWORD

The Davis Mountains region was really wild in the Nineties and later, when we had those great gatherings at the old mountain ranches; and those famous camping-out trips; and the big bear and panther hunts.

When the big game began to disappear in the West Texas Mountains we commenced to hunt bear and panther in the Moggollons and the Black Range in New Mexico. When we first settled in the Davis Mountains in 1884 the bear were so very numerous that the women-folks made bread out of bear-oil; and the old Pioneers used deer and antelope meat for the table and the chuck-wagons. Panthers were so thick in the canyon in 1890 where the Evans ranch was established, that it was called Panther Canyon. Eight boys and one girl were raised up in this canyon. Old long-eared hounds were also raised, as well as children; and George W. Evans and his eight sons hunted bear and panther as a great family hunting team; and the children and grand-children are all hunters and keep up the strains of the old hunting dogs. Always new packs are coming on.

Many of these old hunts were written up by Kid Billy, the scribe of the family, for newspapers; then the writer turned in many hunting stories to various magazines, signing his real name. These have been preserved thru the years and are now being presented in book form. Articles by H. E. Crowley, J. C. Powell, Joe and Dub Evans have been used.

Illustrated by Linda Faulk, grand-daughter of

Will F. Evans

At Old "Rock Pile"

MOONLIGHT IN THE WILDS.
FROM BORDER SKYLINES

By

Congressman. HATTON W. SUMNERS

MOONLIGHT IN THE WILDS

Oh, the joy of the camper's life,
Away from the world's bitter strife
In the heart of the kindly hill,
Where nature sways its scepter still;
And gives to each the soul of a child,
This camping out in the rugged wild.

What care we now for worldly fame—
A tinsel title, a gilded name?
Can the music of the Masters thrill
Like music from the hill?
Can the glow of the city's light
Take the place of the stars at night?
Can the mansion, with its spacious halls,
Appeal to us like the towering walls
That lift sheer up from the valley's edge,
Rock on rock and ledge on ledge?

Was such a thing as Saw Tooth grand
Ever carved by sculptor's hand?
Does man's work, of any style,
Thrill and charm like old "Rock Pile,"
At whose base tonight we camp—
The sky our tent, the moon our lamp,
And which, upon its rugged face,
Bears the tales of a vanished race
That around these stones lived and wrought,
And in these mountains, loved and fought?

Can the arts of the cities fair
Bring down their streets, this mountain air,
That soothes away from the tired brain,
All its care and high-wrought strain,
And lays us down on nature's breast,
Just to rest, just to rest?

ONE OF THE BED WAGONS

Annual Bear Hunt at Nunn Ranch

By Kid Billy

In Pecos Valley News

Three large hunting parties, all "loaded for b'ar;" all coming from different directions, but headed for the same place, reached the Nunn gate near the bottom of the Hill at the same time. In the crowd from Valentine was the noted John S. Bonner, Editor of K. Lamity's Harpoon, the guest of John Z. Means.

That night in the old log cabin at the Nunn ranch and around the camp fire before daylight, the sparkling wit and the musical talent of this brilliant writer kept the whole crowd laughing and encoring.

There were three full packs of bear dogs; Jones & Finley's pack; John Z. Means pack, and the Evans pack; all three packs were of the cold-nosed, long-eared pot-licker type; and meant sudden death for any bear which left a trail under 24 hours old; so the guns were all primed for the real sport of the year in the very heart of the bear hunting country.

Before the east had begun to pale, the mounted hunters were headed for Horse Hollow, a step gash in the mesa which runs into Madera Canyon above Buck Knob Trail and Jim Nunn Hollow and other short gorges. The whole country is rough and hard to negotiate across the north tributaries of Madera, and next to impossible on portions on the south side.

One party went down Horse Hollow and another followed the "back-bone" on the east of this canyon. All met and went down Madera to the mouth of Jim Nunn Hollow, thense up the divide east of Jim Hollow for a mile and a half, then we saw a bear start up the big mountain on the west and head north. One dog was made to see the bear, even at this great distance and two other dogs followed him to where they picked up the bear's trail. The rest of the dogs were taken down Madera as fast as our horses could run and we reached the place where the bear had crossed Madera about three minutes after the bear had crossed going east. Ote and Zee Finley were just ahead of the party with the dogs. Zee killed the bear as it started up out of the creek. Every member of the party who had seen the bear got to the spot just as Zee fired the fatal shot. That was bear No. 1.

The next morning the early dawn caught us far up in the high and heavily timbered mountains near Pine Springs. This time some of the girls went along; (and those girls in the "open range" days, though they rode a side saddle, they had some of the old Pioneer fire in their veins; they were usually in at the kill.) The girls went with Mr. Ote, Joe and Sam and Bill Jones with the dogs up the crooked canyon known as "Elbow," which empties into Brown Canyon before it goes into Madera.

The main party had split into squads of three or four for several miles in the vicinity of Pine Springs. The dogs struck a hot trail in Elbow and crowded the bear so closely he had to top out near Pine Springs where he expected to cross over and make his get-away down one of the steep mountain sides on the upper Limpia; but his keen nose and alert ears warned him that too many men were stationed across his path, so he tumbled off back down Elbow again; a bear does not run down hill, he just rolls and tumbles till he hits bottom; and no horse or dog has ever yet been able to beat a bear to the bottom of a hill in rough country. They sometimes jump off a bluff 75 feet high hitting the ground like a fur ball; they roll till they get on their feet, and they are gone again, none the worse for the wear.

All old experienced bear hunters have seen this feat performed right before their own eyes.

After long and tedious waiting, the men and girls on the lookouts rode back into camp. On the long, hot chase after the bear the dogs had gotten so hot and dry they had ceased to bark, and had also lost the bear's trail as he jumped from rim to rim back into Elbow, but they finally struggled back to where they were gathered up by the men who started out with them. About this time the hunters met a man coming up Brown Canyon who said he had seen the bear and shot at it and said the bear was headed for Nations Canyon, one of the most inaccessible canyons in the Davis Mountains. Joe and Bill Jones and Dr. Penquite topped out east and went nearly to Nations Canyon, thence back into Madera where the dogs had a monster bear at bay in the rough boulders on the side of a mountain.

Dr. Penquite had a high-powered 405 calibre gun; he shot the bear in the head and the ball passed through the skull and the entire body, coming out at the bear's thigh. It was the largest bear ever killed in the Davis Mountains with the exception of the huge Silver Tip killed in Merrill Canyon. This was bear No. 2.

The third and last day, while the stars were still a twinkling, we were again in the saddle. The route lay up "House Log" Canyon; across over into "Saw Mill." Near the head of Saw Mill the united packs struck a hot trail which led them east through a country too rough to ride, so our party followed the old saw mill road up through Briggs Spring Gap and headed north toward Pine Springs as we kept in hearing of the dogs.

Others of the party went down Saw mill following the old road which led back towards the Upper U up and U down ranch. But their choice was sure a good one; they made better time. I was with the party which topped out; and we really risked our necks through the thick brush and over boulders as thick as they could lie. We could hear the dogs at bay about a mile to the west and beneath us. Zee and Huling left their horses with Lee and I and made off down the steep mountain side where a horse couldn't even stand up, headed for the bayed-up bear. But they reached the tree just one minute too late as Mr. Ote, Joe, Sam and Ell, who had came up the Canyon out of Saw Mill, reached the tree first and killed the bear. This was bear No. 3, which ended the great hunt.

Will F. Evans

Linda Faulk

A ferocious Black Bear

A Bear Hunt in H O Canyon

By KID BILLY

In Pecos Valley News

Steve Pate and Wallace Smith, two Long X cowpunchers were batching in the old H O adobe house in H O Caynon when bear were still plentiful.

Joe and I, who were living at the Nunn Ranch, got word from these boys that a fresh bear track had been seen in Deserted Canyon, a thickly timbered basin near the west base of Saw Tooth mountain.

From this lonely old cabin in this mountain pass, we four cowboys led the pack of bear dogs out up H O Hill before daylight. The dogs struck a hot trail at the head of Deserted Canyon and followed it around the foot of the mountains through a jungle of underbrush underneath the tall pines where the boulders were thick, and some of them as high as a horse. The trail led through a gap on the north side of Saw Tooth and took a straight course east off down the mountain side, crossed a wide, timbered valley, and on to a rough mountain north of Cinnamon Canyon.

Joe and Wallace followed in the wake of the dogs; Steve and I took a course to the right to intercept the bear if he went that way; for if he ever toped out on Cinnamon Ridge ahead of us he would head for the real bear country where he would get away.

The silence in this great mountain forest is one of the most impressive experiences a man ever felt. After an hour or more of riding, stopping and listening, not a sound of the trailing dogs could be heard. Steve bid me good bye and started out to ride his steel trap line, and I headed back for the Nunn Ranch, thoroughly disappointed.

Joe and Wallace in the meantime, had been staying up as close to the dogs as they possibly could, considering the course they had to take, for a bear always picks the thickest brush and the roughest country in which to make his get-away.

The dogs finally treed the bear in a rough canyon, and as they were then very hot and dry, they ceased to bark for awhile as they kept sentinel under the tree in which their prey was perched. (It was probably at this very period while the dogs were not barking, that Steve and I rode so near them but heard nothing.)

The bear was in a tree on the mountainside directly below where the boys dismounted. They both fired at the same time; the bear turned holds a loose and nearly fell, but hugged the tree again more tightly; again the boys fired, and down he fell amongst the dogs, and though mortally wounded the bear was knocking the charging, yelping dogs right and left, and had to be shot again before he was finished.

Joe reached the Nunn Ranch at 12:15 with his dead bear and we lived the chase and its final success all over again.

Will F. Evans.

Shipping From Kent

By Kid Billy

In Pecos Valley News

The EV herd of 800 steers moved out of our China tank horse pasture just as the sun showed its rising reflection beyond Borracho Peak, headed for the shipping point at Kent.

Kent was reached by 4 P. M., where we found W. D. Cowan & Son already there with a herd of cattle which we helped to tally out and load, while our herd was being held outside, waiting for the use of the pens.

The Y6 herd of 840 steer yearlings had reached Thorne Lake a couple of miles west of Kent and were being tallied out.

E. L. Jones had already reached Kent with his yearlings which were ready for the cars. Bill Jones and C. O. Finley were on hand with 100 heifer yearlings. These small bunches were put in the back pens; the Y6 steers were put in the two middle pens and ours were put in the big front pen. Ours were 1's, 2's, 3's and 4's, and we put them in the outside pen so that we could turn them out and classify them early the next morning.

We all went to Thorne Lake where our wagons were camped for the night. We did not have any "Night hawk," (the night horse wrangler), so we had to take turns in herding the remuda that night. Just about sunrise as the last horse had been caught and saddled, a group of men with Thompson and Bohart drove up from Kent and informed us that our steers had stampeded in the night, and the entire herd of EV steers with the exception of a few cripples and a dead one or two were very much absent from that front pen which had been flattened out on its entire east side.

Our big outfit of men quickly organized and rode in a gallup as we scattered and swung out toward the west and south side of the big Kent Pasture. By 9 o'clock we had the stampeded herd back to the round-up ground near the Kent stock pens, but in the wide drive we had picked up many X cattle, so after changing horses we had to cut out all of these cattle before we could begin to tally ours out.

We really saw west Texas cowboys in action that day. Our steers were all classed while the Jones, Finleys and Y6's were loading out their cattle. There was a large bunch of men to pen the steers as fast as they could be classed; men to load; men to tally and count out carload lots; men to keep the cattle passing into the back pens as fast as the boys could use them.

Between 7 A. M. and 5 P. M. a big pasture was rounded up, our 800 steers were taillied and classed, a big bunch of X cattle were cut out, and the 1800 or more steers had been put on the cars. Then the bills of sales and checks were made out and the steers left the west for good.

Will F. Evans.

Branding on the Y6 Range

By KID BILLY

In Pecos Valley News

It is the rare privilege of the cowboy to un-roll his tarp on the sweet smelling turf and gaze in peaceful quiet at the myriad of twinkling stars; to feel the indefinable touch of the daylight air; to see the east throw its kaleidoscopic colors across the firmament in colors no man can paint, as the orb of day heralds its coming light.

To sip the coffee fresh from the pot, to have a zest for real old chuck-wagon fare. To stretch up the ropes around 150 cow-ponies, rope them out till the Foreman yells; "Every body got?" To witness the bridling and the saddling of 25 ponies for the regular morning drive, with many horses bucking and all hands whooping it up, "Hang 'em in 'im." To go off in a high gallop like a troup of cavalry men, over the bushes and the badger holes and rank grasses still wet with the morning dews that sparkle like a million diamonds in the rays of the rising sun.

To be dispersed in squads or singly along the way by the wagon boss to cover all the country to be driven that morning, till the men have spread out like a fan, to converge to the common center, which is the round-up ground, the main watering place for the cattle on that strip of country.

To see the hundreds of white-faced cattle in a great herd and hear the constant bawling of the herd, with the throaty bellow of a bull throwing his challenge to all bulls within hearing, and smell the cattle smell of the milling animals. It all gets in the blood of the cowboy, and is a part of his life.

A couple of boys usually stand watch over the herd while the rest of the boys head for the remuda which the horse wrangler has brought in from the grass. Everybody changes off onto his best trained mounts; and if chuck has not been called, they head back to the round up, the cattle are moved out aways from the watering place; here the Foreman gives the orders as to who will ride in to cut out the strays, the unbranded calves with their mothers, and any shipping stuff which is being held to be thrown into holding pastures till market time.

All calves of different brands have been cut into different

bunches. These are penned in the separate corrals; the strays and shipping cattle are thrown into their respective pastures and the boys head for the chuck wagon for the noon meal which is called dinner. There is no formality in the cowboy circle, though few men have more natural gallantry and consideration for the other fellow than the range raised cowboy; his ways are as broad as the country he rides.

The real work of the day commences when 300 or more wild and kicking calves, weighing from 300 to 400 pounds have to be laid on their sides by the husky flankers or tailers, after the irons have become red hot in a branding fire.

In a big out-fit there is usually three sets of flankers, two branders, two markers (In this day of high pressure Franklin products, and the de-horning processes on all steer calves, 2 more men are required; a de-horner and a "doper") one man with book and pencil to keep tally of each calf branded; with two ropers busy dragging them up as fast as the boys can handle them; but in a close pen where all the calves are of the same brand, where the calves have been separated from the cows, the ropers are dispensed with; the calves are thrown by tailing flanking, or jawing down; two men to the calf.

When the sun sinks to rest, the tired old boys, after a good wash and a hearty meal, stretch out full length on the un-rolled, welcome beds, and let Dame Nature restore to them the pep and energy for the coming morning and another strenous day, just like yesterday, but always different.

These thoughts, which are reminiscent of the round ups of the open range days, are fresh in mind, from their recent enactment to the letter on the Y6 "work" just closed.

Ell and I with our horses and a "hot-roll' wrapped around the middle of one of them, bore west till we reached Chispa, on the G. H. & S. A., where the whole Y6 out-fit, cowboys, women and children and all were congregated to celebrate the beginning of the annual Y6 work.

The nights were given over to merry making, listening to fine music, dancing and eating the dainty refreshments prepared by the girls till near midnight.

The remnant of the cattle left on the Williams side of the Railroad were worked the first day, and the round-up thrown down to the Wilson place near the Rio Grande. In seven days we branded 2226 calves, and they were dandy big fellows too.

The chuck prepared by two Mexican cooks, and all kinds of

sweets and dainties by the ladies, were but a repetition of the good things we have to eat at the old Bloys Cow Boy Camp Meeting each year. Generous rains fell all over the range; the "slickers" were used many times. All the way round it was one continuous round of work and pleasure, long to be remembered.

Will F. Evans.

A Goat Roping Match

By KID BILLY

In Pecos Valley News

On July 4, 1905, the Means and Evans and a delegation from Valentine headed by Jim Browning drove into the mountain glen where the beautiful old ranch home of C. O. Finley sets like a diamond in a ring of a cluster of granite spires.

Here we met the families of Bill Jones from the Kelly Ranch (which was then the Bill Jones Head-quarter ranch) and C. O. Finley and family and friends. The harness was stripped from the mule teams, the saddles from the cow ponies which were turned loose to wallow on the green turf, shake their steaming sides and fill up on the crow-foot grama in C. O.'s horse "trap."

It was a real ranch get-together, with music, laughter and good cheer; barbecue with all the trimmings, cakes, ice cream and lemonade and a (social gathering which was enjoyed in those old open range days with an intensity which is seldom ever equaled in this day and time.)

Eleven wild Mexican goats had been gathered up from the hills and placed in a goat proof corral. When the sun had begun to dip towards the west and the shadows of the crags began to lengthen over the valley, the men and boys, old men and young headed for the corrals and saddled their cow ponies in preparation for the great sport of roping and tying a running, dodging goat, one of the most amusing of all roping contests, and also one of the most difficult to perform.

Men with flowing beards, small boys with their light weight ropes, cow boys in their prime; they all had their chance to perform before the hilarious groups atop the fences, hooting or cheering in spontaneous enjoyment. Then came cigar races; and to see one of those old fellows, who had never had a cigar in their mouth's in their lives, race their pony up to a cigar on the ground, jump off, light the cigar and come back to the starting line as fast as their ponies could run, puffing away on the cigar was too funny for words. Then boots and shoes were placed in a heap some distance away, when a free for all bare-footed race was indulged in by men and women and girls and boys; of course not a one of the contestants found their own shoes or boots, nor a one that would fit, or a pair that would match.

There were sack races, one of the most ridiculous of all stunts; it results in only tumbles and laughter. Another great feast for supper; then beautiful music by talented members of the crowd; then dancing till midnight; then sweet dreams; a sunrise over the lofty summit of Mt. Livermore; a breakfast no king ever ate; then the trek to the respective ranches far away.

(The old horse and buggy days are gone forever, but sweet memory carries the events of the past along abreast of the times of to-day.)

Will F. Evans.

Scared

Panther

Linda Faulk.

A West Texas Panther Chase

By WILL F. EVANS

In Stock-Farmer

Leaving the EV ranch about One P. M. eight of the Means and Evans hunters cut through the mountains with the combined packs of hounds headed for Borracho Canyon, a steep gash which heads up near Borracho Peak, (Now in the pasture of Bea Wallace) while Lee drove the four mule wagon loaded with beds, camp outfit and chuck. We had 16 hounds and the white bull dog Tessie.

Night comes early in this black defile, and the sun goes down much ahead of the clock, for it gets dark long before it does on the prairie. It was nearly a quarter of a mile up the canyon to the large cistern from which we would have to carry our water for the camp.

John Means, as he sat by the camp fire, with the inky darkness all around, restrospected for the benefit of the boys who were going to have to make another trip up the canyon for more water for breakfast; "Boys, you know history repeats itself every 20 years. Well sir, right here on this very spot, just 20 years ago to a night, H. M. Newman (At that time one of the owners of the MF Ranch, now the X Ranch) and a company of men hit camp after dark when one man was dispatched up the creek to get some water to cook with. The man reached down to dip up his bucket full of water and a panther landed on him and clawed him pretty badly."

History did repeat itself concerning the panther, for a panther did visit the cistern the very night we camped in the canyon. We were in the saddle before daylight and the dogs which had all been untied, struck the trail at once, making the walls of the black canyon echo and re-echo with their animated barking.

This is a "box" canyon and there is only one trail out of it which picks a precarious shelf on the side of the main canyon wall at its head. We had to trust to the night eyes of our ponies to carry us safely out over this narrow trail in the dark.

The trail led out across the mesa and along the rim rock which walls the mountains for miles on their western side. We all rode as fast as we could ride over the boulders and the sharp spears of the lechugillas which were very thick on the ground. The scent was so fresh that the dogs never lost it till the panther left it in mid-air as he jumped off the bluff into Hackberry canyon which cuts into the mesa just east of Borracho Peak. When we reached the bluff and looked off into the canyon not a sound could be heard.

We were as puzzled as the dogs as to where the panther was, but we knew he was somewhere in that canyon. Presently one of us chanced to focus his vision directly under a large tree which had a clearing as large as a room down below it. Right in the center of this clearing crouched a huge panther, and even at this great distance on the south side of the canyon, we could see that he was a big one. It was a freak of nature that the panther was hidden from the dogs, but not from us across the canyon; the rays of the sun just for a moment, had exposed the panthers position to us. Presently Belle came directly down through the cedar break, but she turned off down the hill without seeing or smelling the big beast which was crouched so near her; but presently one of the younger dogs headed straight to the panther, when the big beast with the agility of its kind, leaped from cliff to cliff and on up to the top. The pup was so scared he never even gave a yelp to give the other dogs a clue as to the panther's whereabouts. But Blue was coming along on top the cliff headed towards the fleeing panther, when the dog and panther collided. Blue had the cool courage of the real old hound so he attacked the large beast with such fury that the panther jumped 20 feet in the air, and with long leaps, his tail high in the air was soon out of sight. However Blue picked up the trail and soon put the panther to bay on a shelf about 20 feet from the summit. Blue barked so vigorously that the panther took fright and leaped clear to the bottom of the main cliff. Lee and Huling out-rode the rest of us as we circled the head of the gorge; they were followed closely by Joe and Sam and the four of them overtook Blue as the dog was following the brink of the cliff still barking at the panther which was leaping from boulder to boulder along beneath the bluff, headed towards Borracho Peak and the roughs which contain many caves and crevices where the old panther knew he could get away.

The four boys all left their horses at the same time and ran to the edge of the bluff and looked off just as the panther came into view beneath them. Four shots fired almost as one, sent four steel-jacket bullets into the panther killing him instantly. The panther was a big one and had been depredating on X colts and calves. The skin was sent to H. H. Adams of Dallas.

Bear Hunting From the Upper Locke

U UP AND U DOWN RANCH

By KID BILLY

From The Pecos Valley News

Alf Means was running the U Up and Down when bear were very numerous. We pulled some real hunts from this old ranch headquarters in the hills where the high peaks of the Davis Mountains encircle it about.

By day-light the Evans and Means pack of hounds were close at heel as Uncle Alf led the way down Madera Canyon. By sunrise the two packs opened up on two bear trails, one pack running south and the other north. My father followed his dogs which went south and Uncle Alf and I rode north after the other pack where the mountains were straight up and down, and the brush and boulders made the riding very dangerous; we topped out just above where Horse Hollow cuts the great wall into Madera, and directly under the rim ahead of us the dogs had a brown bear up a tree; the brush was so very thick that we did not see the bear till we were right on the brink of the cliff. Uncle Alf beat me to the draw and hit the bear a dead shot.

The bear fell like a huge brown ball amongst the dogs, and as they sunk their teeth in his fur, they were almost half way down the steep mountain-side before we could reach them as we slid over the pine-needles; so there was nothing else to do but for one of us to roll the bear on to the bottom of the hill, and the other to climb back out and find a way off with the horses. I took this job of climbing out. Leading my Uncle's horse, I made my way as fast as possible along the "back-bone," when a bunch of black-tailed deer jumped out in front of me and went stiff-legged off the mountain to the south; when they topped a little elevation they all stopped and looked back at me. The temptation was too great; I jumped off and took quick aim at a big buck; he hit the ground like a beef shot in the head. I bled this buck and went down into the main canyon where I found Uncle Alf resting by the side of this unusual specimen of bear which he had just finished dressing. This bear was brownish colored, with a sandy tinge to his hair; one of the few speciments of its kind ever killed in the Davis Mountains.

When we rode up the canyon for a few miles we found my father had killed a large black bear, and only had to run him a short ways till the bear treed.

We rode into the ranch while the shadows of the morning were still long. After the ladies prepared us a real old ranch dinner, we proceeded to skin the deer and fleece the two bears. While we were doing this we heard some shouts from two well-known voices, as Berry Hues from McAnelly's Bend, and Wallace Smith, foreman of the X ranch came riding up on two X horses. These boys were wild with delight in our successful hunts; and were planning to go with us on another bear hunt the next morning. These boys were both of the daredevil type; and neither one of them had ever killed a bear.

By day-light we were headed up Saw Mill, and by sun-up the dogs struck a trail leading out thru Briggs Spring Gap and over into the head of Limpia. We were seasoned bear hunters and took ordinary caution in picking our way off down the east slopes of Livermore; but these reckless boys rode like wild Indians thru the brush and down the rock-slide; Wallace was riding old Long Brown of the Nunn Ranch; and Berry was riding a large mare of Uncle Alf's; Wallace was in the lead, and when he reached the bottom of the hill his way was blocked by a chasm cut in the solid rock; this wild rider jabbed the spurs into old Brown, and the great old horse cleared the wide gash in a mighty leap which has perhaps never been equaled in any place anywhere else on earth. Berry tried the same treatment on the old mare, but she balked absolutely and finally; which certainly saved Berry from a tragical death in the depths of that mountain gorge.

The thicket and boulders around the head of the gorge made the way so nearly impassable that Berry was a long time getting thru; and before he reached the tree where the bear was at bay, he heard the crack of Wallace's rifle; and so did we, as we reached the scene of the dead bear and the milling dogs and the grinning Wallace right on Berry's heels; and mad! In all of our lives, we had never seen as mad a man as Berry was; and had these boys not been life-long friends, born and raised on the bank of the Colorado, there would have been a man-killing as well as a bear killing, in that wild spot; for the invectives Berry used, and the names he called Wallace for being fool enough to jump his horse across that gorge, was something awful to hear.

It was a long climb out, and a long way to the ranch; on the way back, we convinced Berry that the mountains were full of bear; and many of them much bigger than the one Wallace had killed; and after a good meal at the ranch; he was all pepped up for another hunt the next morning; and he got his bear.

Will F. Evans.

(26)

Dr. Locke Changes His Mind

By KID BILLY

From The Pecos Valley News

This young doctor had just come in from Concord, N. H. to spend a vacation on his daddy's ranches in the Davis Mountains.

We were just planning a bear hunt from the Upper Ranch when Doc showed up. He was togged out in all of his Wild West parapheralia, and rode like the best of us till we got after a bear in the real roughs in the Pine Springs country, then we lost him and he lost us.

This bear was a "running bear;" he would not tree, no matter how close the dogs crowded him; and nearly every one of us got a shot at him on the long chase.

Finally, Uncle Alf and Joe and I made a fast run to a point of advantage where we left our horses and rushed to the edge of the bluff about the time the running bear came into view several hundred yards below us; Uncle Alf and Joe and I were all firing at the fleeing bear; and we hit him every time; and each time we would call out; "I hit him; I hit him:" but he got to his feet after each fall and kept running till he rounded a point out of sight where he went into a cave. When we got to the mouth of the cave, which was not more than 2 feet in diameter, the bear had left a wide belt of blood as he wormed his way into the narrow passage. The cave seemed to be very deep and we could see nor hear anything in its depths; so we disappointedly called off the barking dogs and rode on back to the ranch; no man in his right mind will go into a narrow cave with a wounded bear; so we did not try it. When we reached the ranch late in the day, the other boys were all there eating dinner, and with them, Dr. Locke, who had made his way back over a cattle trail into the ranch.

When we told our story of the wounded bear which we left in the cave, the Doc went up into the air; and he really dressed us down for not bringing in that bear; he said he knew the bear was lying back in there dead; and if he had been there he would have crawled right in and dragged the bear out. We just humped up and took it with a grin; stating that you would not catch either of us going in to drag out a wounded bear.

(27)

The next morning the dogs struck a trail near the head of Saw Mill and only ran the bear a short ways when they put him up a tree, where McAnelly shot him out, but it was not a death-shot; the bear hit the ground fighting; he was slashing dogs right and left; and I have never heard such a mighty roar as this small bear gave out; he really made the bluffs echo; it looked as if he might kill several of our good dogs which were so close to the fighting bear that it was nearly impossible to shoot the bear without killing a dog; Joe finally rushed right in and placed his gun against the bear's body and shot him dead.

When the melee had quieted down we looked around for Doc, who came cautiously riding up, his face as white as a sheet, exclaiming, "Is he dead yet; now, you wouldn't catch me going into a cave with an animal that can give out a roar like that."

We had evened up with the Doc; and he respected us from then on out. He was a very congenial fellow to be around. He has been dead many years.

Will F. Evans.

Peter Clark McFarlane Gets His Picture of a Treed Bear

(The first Photographer ever to do this stunt in the Davis Mountains)

By KID BILLY

From The Pecos Valley News

The old bear hunters left the Nunn Ranch bright and early with the famous writer for Collier's, hoping against hope that the noted fellow could stay on a horse long enough to reach a treed bear and get a snap-shot before the bear jumped out.

On the second day out, Joe and Sam and Edwin Fowlkes, with their three packs scoured the country from Pine Springs, down Elbow and Brown; while I was dispatched with McFarlane, Tom Cherry-holmes, Jim Farmer and others to guard the high gaps on Madera and Nation's Canyon. On the way down one of these long, narrow "back-bones" which divides Madera and Nations, Jim Farmer's horse throwed a shoe ;and as the horse's hoof had been rasped off almost to the quick in the leveling process in fitting the shoe, the poor horse was just walking on three feet; and as Mr. Farmer was a very large man, we were right up against a problem; but I told Mr. Farmer that a fellow by the name of Carmack had taken up some land in this vicinity and had built a cabin on the bluff not far ahead of us; and that there might possibly be a shoeing out-fit there; and as luck would have it, there were horse shoes of the right size, and nails to put on the shoe; I shod the limping horse, and we went on our way rejoicing. Big Jim thought that was the most remarkable incident which could ever happen, to find a horse-shoeing out-fit out in this wildest of wild regions.

We rode out onto all the high points and listened till our ears got sore; but never a sound of dogs; along about noon I told the boys that the dogs evidently turned back towards Livermore if they did strike a trail; so we dejectedly took the back-trail south.

When we got within about a half mile of the old Prude Ranch, one of the highest ranches in Texas, we got the fright of our lives; we were confronted by Mrs. Edwin Fowlkes, who was screaming and swinging her sun-bonnet around her head; we knew that some of the boys had happened to a terrible tragedy; and we all turned white with apprehension. But when she came nearer she shouted out; "The boys have the bear in a tree; he may jump out any minute; they are in Brown Canyon; we must get Mr. McFarlane there as quick as possible."

And boy, was that a relief? A team of mules had already been hitched to a buckboard, and the eager photographer and writer was ushered into the buggy, and away the driver went with him. Luck would have it; the Fort Davis road led right by within a short distance of where the bear was treed, where several snap-shots were taken before the bear was dispatched with a bullet. He had been kept in the tree for several hours.

This fine man was one of the "gamest" guests we ever had on any of our hunts; being un-used to riding, he must have suffered tortures from stiffness and soreness, but he never whimpered, and would not ride a foot in a car while he was on that hunt. (We had just gotten our first Automobiles which were fearfully, but not so wonderfully made.)

Will F. Evans.

Rob Brings 'em Back Alive

By Kid Billy

From The Pecos Valley News

We struck a bear trail about the head of Road Hollow and we rode as fast as we could ride over country which was comparably easy-going till we reached the roughs around Pine Springs and the Head of Elbow.

This was one of the hardest days we had ever experienced in trying to keep in hearing of the dogs; they probably got on two trails and split up; but we lost out in connecting with either pack, and rode dis-couragedly back to the Upper Ranch where we gathered around the chuck-wagon and talked over our hard luck, and wondering where the dogs had gone.

Because it was late in the morning before the dogs started anything, it was beginning to get very warm; and a dog which is suffering from heat and thirst, seldom ever barks after the game is treed; the dogs just lie down at the base of the tree and keep a silent watch on the treed bear, waiting patiently for the hunter to come with the rifle and shoot the varmint out; then they give lusty tongues of dog-joy.

I was with two of the boys and we hunted out all the country in the region of Pine Springs, and climbed out on all the high points overlooking Elbow, listening and listening for the lost dogs; but not a sound could we ever hear; so we gave it up as a bad job; but we gave up too soon.

Rob Perkins, who had been raised in these mountains, and had followed a pack of hounds ever since he could ride a horse, was not far behind us; but he was a more thorough hunter than we had been; he rode just a little further out on one of those identical points which we had just left, dis-mounted and stepped to the edge of the bluff, and directly under him, in the top of a pine tree, sat a huge black bear; peeping a little closer, Rob saw two bear cubs crouched in the forks just above the old bear; she was standing guard between her cubs and the dogs; leaning further over, Rob saw the dogs, several of the pack, lying at the base of the tree, and not a one of them making a sound.

This is where Rob used his hunter's instinct, and his desire to capture those cubs alive. He slipped quietly back from the edge of the bluff and found a break where he could clamber down; then he stealthily approached the tree and got within close range of the old bear and cut loose on her. At the crack of his rifle bed-lam broke out amongst the dogs which attacked the fallen bear in a body; but she was entirely dead when Bob reached her. He had already prepared himself with tying strings to use on the cubs; it was no small task to scale the pine tree up to its first limb; but after that the going was good.

How he managed to capture both of these cubs, tie short sticks in their mouths, tie up their feet and get to the bottom with them, nobody but Rob will ever know. He could not have thrown either one of the cubs down ahead of him, as the dogs would have killed them instantly.

Anyway, this kid, still in his teens, came riding into the ranch with two live cubs in his arms and the old bear's fleece tied to his saddle. And did we feel bad about how this boy had succeeded where we had failed? Fearless Rob is ranching in Arizona now. Still a hunter.

Will F. Evans.

Roping Lions For Fun?

By G. W. EVANS

From Western Live Stock
September, 1932.

Deep snow and bitterly cold weather greeted Dr. Calvin when he came out from New York for a lion hunt in the Beaverhead country. But this did not dampen the doctor's ardor or interfere in any way with the plans that had been made for the expedition.

On the night of his arrival the necessary preparations were made for a pack trip and we started out early the next morning. The first day we established camp near Jordan Canyon, about 20 miles from Beaverhead ranch headquarters. Throughout our first day's hunting we never saw a cat track, although there were lots of deer. The next morning, however, our dogs, Old Brownie, Little Brownie and four pups, which were new at the hunting game, hit a cat trail. There turned out to be two of the cats, the dogs jumped them after following the trail for some distance. One went down Jordan Canyon and the other up, the dogs separating to follow. The cat which I followed soon treed, so I shot him with a pistol and went to find the other boys and the dogs. They had a cat at bay in a hole in the rock on the west rim of Jordan Canyon.

We thought by moving some rock we could get near enough to the cat to snare it and tie it up, as Dr. Calvin wanted to take the animal alive. We found this to be a bigger job than we expected, as we had nothing with which to move the large rocks except our hands and some sticks. With little progress being made, we decided it was necessary to send to camp for a spade and an axe.

While waiting for the necessary tools, we heard Little Brownie barking off to the north. With the axe and spade we succeeded in moving enough rocks to get close enough to the cat to snare and tie it up after pulling it out of the hole.

Little Brownie had been gone for four hours, so, leaving the boys, I went to hunt for the dog, carrying the dead cat tied to my saddle behind and the live one up in front of me.

About a quarter of a mile north I came upon Little Brownie's tracks in the snow following a lion track. Immediately putting the other dogs on the trail, I went back to find the rest of the party. Not being able to locate them, I unloaded the dead and live cats and went back to find Dick Etheredge who was accompanying us on the trip. The doctor had gone back to camp by this time, so we decided to follow the trail to see what the dogs were doing. After a half mile we stopped to listen and, from the barking of the dogs, we could tell they were at bay.

We found the lion in the top of a pinon tree before we reached the dogs, and immediately sent back to camp for Dr. Calvin and some additional ropes and chains. Little Brownie was about a hundred yards farther on and had another lion up a pine tree. The dog kept going from tree to tree, and, I suppose, had succeeded in that manner in keeping two lions at bay for four or five hours.

Upon the return of Dick and the doctor we held council and decided it was such a late hour that the best thing we could do would be to shoot one of the lions and try to tie the other. Dr. Calvin shot and killed the one in the pine tree and we proceeded to get some ropes on the other. Dr. Calvin first climbed the tree with a lariat rope and a long, light stick in his hand. With a loop of the rope hung over a fork on the end of the stick he tried to place the noose over the lion's head. The tree was thick with foliage and Dr. Calvin was unsuccessful in roping his quarry. He came down to make room for me to try my hand at getting the rope on a real live mountain lion— the first attempt of my lifetime. Somehow, in the commotion that followed, the rope came off and the lion was loose on the ground with the dogs in hot pursuit. For safety the lion soon went up another tree and I was right after him with a rope and stick. I succeeded in placing the rope around his neck again and there was a repetition of the first performance. Our lariat ropes were hard and stiff from moisture, so it was hard to draw them down around the lion's neck so they would hold. With the rope off the second time the lion tried to make another tree but the dogs would not let him. We were all in the mill together, but luckily Dick placed a loop securely around the infuriated lion's neck. There was some quick action in keeping the dogs off the lion while we stretched him out and tied him. However, we finally managed this after his feet were securely tied together.

We put a stick cross-ways in his mouth and tied it over the top of his head and around his nose and chin so that he could not bite. Thus tied, we loaded him onto my horse across the saddle in front of me and returned to camp. There we placed a colar and chain on the lion and released him from his other bondages.

Near where we tied the lion, we discovered a kill. It was a young deer and was only partly eaten. We decided that if there were more than two lions, and we thought there were, as the two we had taken so far had both been males, that the others would return in the night to the freshly killed deer. Next morning the deer carcass had been moved. The dogs trailed a few hundred feet and we found only the deer skin and bones, indicating by the amount of meat eaten that there was more than one lion left.

The dogs worked hard trying to get the trail straightened out and finally jumped the lions. One went up a tree and the other went back in the direction from which we had just come.

The dogs treed this one finally about a mile from the first lion. As one more live lion was about all we could use, Dr. Calvin shot one out of the tree and we got all the dogs and men together in an attempt to tie the remaining lion. After our successful attempt of the previous evening of lion-tying, we felt less doubtful about this one. Dick was the first to go up the tree and he placed two ropes securely around the lion's neck; Dr. Calvin taking one rope and I the other, pulling the lion out.

I have never seen any animal display more action than a freshly roped lion. He springs, turns, flops and rolls, striking in every direction with claws extended. But after our experience with the cat and lion of the day before, we made short work of tying this one. We then returned to camp with the two lions, one of them very much alive.

We loaded the two live lions on Kitty, a very dependable pack mule. Securely tied, the lions were set in a kiack, a box tied with rope looped in each end to hang over the fork on a pack saddle. Thus they sat facing the mule's head, tied so they could not get out, but biting and spiting at everything that moved.

Being afraid that the mule might pass under a low-hanging tree or otherwise do damage to the lions, I led her all the way to the ranch. We crated the two live lions and shipped them by Express, where they no doubt caused quite a stir among Dr. Calvin's friends, who might have thought these speciments belonged in the jungles of South Africa.

Madera Camp Meetings

By KID BILLY

In Pecos Valley News

(In probably one of the mostly wildly picturesque locations in the entire Davis Mountains these camp meetings were held for a few sessions in the first part of this century and then abandoned. Not even a scar is left on the site now.)

With 14 big mules shod all around, the EV and Y6 outfits with men, women and children left the Y6 Ranch bound for Bill Jones' Kelly Ranch where we were joined by the Jones and Finley delegation and friends.

With horse-back riders in the lead, then the buggies and four-mule hacks followed by the chuck wagons, took the winding road through the foot-hills of the Davis Mountains, passed through lovely Skillman's Grove, the home of the old Blys Cowboy Camp Meeting, and brought our cavalcade at a stop under the beautiful cotton wood trees which surrounded W. Keesey's home in Fort Davis. Here we were joined by this old Pioneer merchant and his wife and her sister. Mr. Keesey established the first General Merchandise store in Ft. Davis in 1873, freighting his supplies by ox-team, then burro, and later mule teams from San Antonio, several hundred miles over a road little more than a cattle trail. He not only furnished the goods, but advanced the money to the cowmen to buy these goods, and carried them on his books till they sold cattle at the far-away markets.

The drive down Limpia with its towering finger crested crags over head, the brightly hued cotton woods, the dark green foliage of the mountain oaks, the paler green of the willows and the many shades of green and gray in the under brush along the way, makes this trek through the mountains one of the most delightful of all over-land trips.

Every turn in the canyon brings to view the beautiful handiwork of God in the sculpturing of the mammoth pillars in the great walls of granite which hem the canyon in.

(At this time only the old government pack-trail led out through Wild Rose Pass through which the Modern paved highway now goes, so we had to buck the boulder-strewn way down the bed of the wild old canyon itself.)

Night overtook us just below the narrows, and we pitched camp for the night by the clear waters of the rippling mountain creek, where the fire-wood lay all about us for the taking, and the crow-foot grama grew flush with the water's edge.

This camping out in the wilds with the towering mountains standing sharp above us in their majestic skylines, made a memorial picnic which none of us ever forgot.

Leaving Limpia Canyon our road led through the foot hills which cluster about the north base of Star Mountain, and on by the Seven Springs Ranch, the McCutcheon head-quarters, then on around the north base of the lofty Timber Mountain, by the W. L. Kingston head-quarters at the mouth of Madera, and then up into the wilds of this mountain gorge itself, where the camp meeting tabernacle graced the little sheltered cove with its white canvas in sharp contrast to the livid green of the timber and the black walls of the canyon.

Here we met several hundred friends, old and new, after a trip which consumed four days and a half. (Now you can make it in four hours and a half.)

The Rev. George W. Truett of Dallas, trained to be a Lawyer, but ordained to be a preacher, plead the Master's cause with a logic and a power so compelling, that he seemed to be speaking directly and personally to each individual who heard his fiery eloquence.

Something long to be remembered was a midnight baptizing by lantern light in one of the many pools of pure water up the canyon where the surface of the pool now black with the mantle of the night, reflected the eerie light of the flickering lanterns as the old cowboy preacher, the Rev. L. R. Millican, led the penitents in waist deep, and plunged them under, while the voices of the choir in this rampart of nature will linger long in our memory to be heard in the grand symphony which connects with the Choir Invisible.

Will F. Evans.

LINDA FAULK

A Panther Chase

By J. C. POWELL

(Old Ft. Davis Hunter)

Fort Davis Dispatch

"Last week while I was out the Mountain (Short Canyon) Ranch I had a little hunt one morning. About 4 A. M. as I was lying on my bed, which was snuggly built on the ground, Old Driver, one of my bear dogs, woke me up by putting his head near me and whinning loud, as much as saying; 'Get up and let us go catch a bear.' I threw the tarp back, saw that old Luna was shining bright, called my trusty cook, and it wasn't long before he had the coffee boiling and ready for me. It was heap stout, and went fine with a good breakfast. I saddled and hopped on Old Comanche, and with nine wolf and bear hounds following, was climbing the lofty mountain out of the canyon.

"All was quiet the first four miles!; only now and then a yelp from some of the young dogs. After getting on top of the big mountain it was almost daylight. The dogs were not far ahead of me when old Driver and Rustler made the mountain-tops ring with their melodious voices, saying; 'Come on, he has been here'; and pretty soon the balance of the pack began putting in their part of the music; and slowly eastward they began to go, making music sweet to hear; but on they went for three miles; and getting off into the flat the trail seemed to get colder; so when they got to the Toyah and Ft. Davis road I loped ahead and found that they were on the back track, as I could plainly see the big tracks of the animal going in the opposite direction; so back we went in a lope to where old Driver first struck the trail, and the dogs all joined in on the right end of the trail.

"Old Driver having been bitten in the leg by two rattlesnakes, and carrying a part of a 30-30 bullet in the other leg, was a little piece behind the pack. He would stop and smell the bushes, then ring out in a loud voice, which was music to any old hunter's ear. On they went into a place where the sun does not shine more than four hours in a day; the trail getting warmer and the dogs making the brush pop as over rough places and down the canyon they went, making the mountain-tops echo with their wild music. I was really riding to them, regardless of sharp snags, and high boulders in my patch.

"Pretty soon I heard them "tree;" and on a big rock was sitting as big a panther as I had ever seen. I 'throwed Old Betsy' down on him and he came rolling off the bluff; and when he struck the ground the dogs all covered him; but he was too dead to make any fight.

"I then took the dogs to some water a short distance way, and after they had drank and cooled off a while, they struck a new trail and away they went. They did not go far till they put another panther to bay on a bluff. I got up close enough to where I could see the hind part of the panther, and old Betsy spoke again. The shot was not vital, and he leaped off the bluff, with the dogs in hot pursuit. It was a fast race for a quarter of a mile, when the dogs overtook the wounded panther, when he turned on them and really put up a nasty fight; but they were too many for him.

"It was about a mile to the top of the mountain where I had left my horse. I was tired and hungry, and my clothes nearly torn off of me. When I got within about one half mile from my horse, the dogs opened up on another trail; and I told them to, 'go for him, old fellows.' They ran about a mile and put this panther up a cedar tree. This was panther number three. Of course old Betsy spoke again, hitting the panther in one fore leg. Down he came right amongst the yelping, fighting dogs, when a fight to the finish ended this panther.

"I sent the three hides off to have them mounted."

(Note: Perhaps no hunter in all the wild and rugged mountain regions, ever rode as recklessly as did Jim Powell after a lobo wolf, a bear, or a panther.)   (Who is now deceased.)

Big Bear Hunt at Rockpile

By H. E. CROWLEY

In The Midland Reporter

This is one time in my life when I would really like to be a descriptive writer. The occasion referred to was a bear hunt in the Davis Mountains.

The good people who live in the Davis Mountains and have ranches in that locality celebrate after this fashion annually.

I was fortunate enough to receive an invitation; and while I had often heard of these chases, and knew by reputation these typical frontiersmen and their wholesouled congeniality, I had absolutely no conception of either the magnitude or the pleasure of the thing. The startling fact about this bear hunt is that the party was composed of more than 80 persons, ranging in ages from six months to seventy-nine years; 250 head of saddle horses and 40 good bear dogs.

There were three chuck-wagons and as many cooks: the way this large crowd was fed and comfortably stored away in tents and under tarps for the night is a thing beyond my ability to describe. The men who accomplished this task with such ease and dispatch, were Messrs. Geo. W. Evans, John Z. Means, Ote Finley, Merritt Finley, W. T. Jones, Reynolds Bros. and others. It was the biggest thing I ever saw.

The camp was struck near the foot of "Old Saw Tooth" at the base of one of the picturesque rock piles, at the Rockpile tank on the Reynolds range. Saw tooth is one of the very lofty peaks of the Davis Mountains, and takes its name from the cragged appearance of its summit and is a marvel of scenic beauty.

Rockpile tank, an artificial lake takes its name from the two small mountains of granite which rise to a height of many feet flush from the floor of the valley. This very spot where our camp was located, for novelty and scenic beauty, in my judgment, is not surpassed even by the famous Garden of the Gods in Colorado.

In this camp at the foot of the rockpiles was matronly ladies, old men, young men, preachers, doctors, lawyers, bankers, merchants, politicians and boys and girls.

Those of us who were met at Kent as we got off the West bound train on the T. & P., were Rev. M. K. Little from Itasca; Rev. John Barcus, Corsicana; Geo. T. and W. D. Beir; O. Smith, Fort Worth; James Butler, Newton Fallis, Clifton; Hon. J. T. Tucker, Taylor County; Ed. Colling, Will Pore, Pecos; Wm. Adkinson, Zee Finley, Roswell; John M. Cowden and myself from Midland.

After spending the first night at Reynolds Bros. ranch seven miles south of Kent, John M. and I were furnished with good horses and rode thru the hills to the camp at Rock Pile, reaching there late that afternoon with a nice black-tailed buck deer each tied on our saddle. (When Ed. Crowley and John M. Cowden came in view of this great camp, Ed. Crowley nudged his companion and said, "John M., we have run up against the real thing this time."

250 saddle horses were enclosed with a "rope corral" and some of the boys who were good with the rope, caught out enough horses to mount the entire group of men who were to go on the bear chase next morning. We staked our horses out for the night; after supper a huge fire was made, and the great throng gathered around it for one of those get-togethers known and experienced only on the frontier. Then Bronco, as "Rev." Jake Cloyd, sung his rollicking "Nigger" songs; then took on a sanctimonious face as he took his text from "De Forth Sams of Judy" and proceeded in tones of "baso profoundo" to make the welkin ring.

Just as the first rays of the morning light began to rise all the hunters were mounted and ready for the first bear chase; the hounds which had been tied up, were all set free, and pandimonium broke loose on the mountain air. Old Brownie, the trusty old bear dog was put in the lead, ahead of all the men; as he never starts anything but a bear. About 8:30 Brownie opened up on a bear trail and the whole pack broke loose and joined him in their wild chorus. Here is where the indescribable part of the chase came in; the sound of the dogs as their voices echoed and re-echoed in the hill-tops, the enthusiasm and excitement of the hunters as they rushed pell-mell over rocks and thru brush, down the mountains, tearing clothes, skinning shins, losing hats, etc., are to me indescribable.

There were two bear at the start this time and when they finally separated, the dogs did the same, each division in hot pursuit of Mr. Bruin. The first one killed was a two year old, and bayed in a cave in the rim rock near the summit of the mountain; the other one in a high pine tree. About two P. M. all hands were back in camp with two bear and three deer.

Again at nightfall we gathered around another huge fire and re-lived our exciting adventures of the chase for the benefit of the ladies and others who stayed in camp. Deserving of special mention, was the beautiful singing of the Misses Slack of Bosque County who rendered sweet music we all enjoyed. We killed two more bear and then broke camp. It was the greatest outing we ever had of any kind, or even heard of.

OTE FINLEY JOHN MEANS

Linda Faulk.

THE OLD SILVER TIP

OFF OF HIS RANGE

Off of His Range

KILLING THE OLD SILVER TIP

By WILL F. EVANS

From The Hunter-Trader-Trapper

The big Silver Tip Bears are exclusive in their tastes, as they can only be found in the highest, the roughest and the most densely timbered mountains of the United States.

In a region of West Texas, known as the Trans-Pecos, or the Big Bend country, lies the beautiful range of mountains known as the Davis Mountains.

The culminating peak of these mountains is known as Mt. Livermore and its height is 8,750 feet above sea level, while a great number of peaks of lesser altitude jut skyward in every direction. All of the canyons of the Davis Mountains have their tributaries starting from the base of this old mountain, which is several miles across and the water that it sheds off its rugged old back is taken into the Rio Grande on the south and the Pecos on the east.

In the good old days when game was plentiful, and so was our time and our money, and the worries of the bill-collectors did not ruffle our brows, or harrass our spirits, we used to have the great bear hunts in the Davis Mountains.

Ten miles northwest of Mt. Livermore lies its rival neighbor, Mt. Saw Tooth, whose back is covered with tall spires of moss-covered cliffs that cleave the heavens in a jagged outline like the teeth of a saw.

Just north of this wonderful mountain on an undulating mesa, two small rock mountains rise flush from the grass-carpeted valley to the height of 200 feet. Big trees about the base of these rock mountains, and peeping up through the crevices, their green foliage against the grey boulders, forms a picture for the gods.

At the southern side of one of these miniature mountains, we pitched camp among the trees; tents were stretched up for the ladies and children, three chuck wagons placed in file, all abreast, with several Mexican cooks to prepare the food royal. Fat beeves are killed, and the many hunters in the crowd usually bring in a buck or two, the first night.

(45)

The old timers, Means, Evans, Jones and Finley, with their families, friends and invited guests form a party of seventy five people, and they have along a great remuda of horses with Mexican night and day herders, and thirty long-eared hounds, hacks, buggies and bed-wagons; that is the way we went about having good times.

When the gay night larks of the cities are just going to bed for the day, before the faintest light has ever touched the east, the cooks are preparing breakfast; the first thing on the fire is a five gallon can of coffee that soon is boiling; while the old boys, one and two and so on, come stiff-legged up to the chuck-box for a cup. They protect their faces with one hand and with the other they dip into the pot and bring a steaming cup of coffee. Breakfast just for the men; roping horses at break of day from a rope corral; horns blowing and horses bucking and dogs a howling, when the cavalcade heads for Livermore.

Up Road Canyon, through the pines and dense under-growth of oaks, pinons, juniper, wild-cherries, mansanitas, etc., we top out around the east slope of Cinnamon Ridge; off into Saw Mill Canyon about the Richmond Place; on up Saw Mill to the north end of Tobe Gap, when the party follows the old deserted Saw Mill road around the side of Livermore up through Brigg's Spring Gap, when pandemonium breaks loose in dog land and twenty five men scattered in squads, each group following a leader; but many there be that start, but few that ever get there, when you start a bear in the Davis Mountains.

After a break-neck pace through the debris of fallen trees and piled-up boulders, I was in the lead of a party of four men on the top of Livermore; with the rocks flying out from under our horses feet as we sheered around the heads of the canyons that led off east towards Ft. Davis.

On the brink of Limpia Canyon we paused for our horses to get their wind, when McAnelly (now deceased) said, "Gosh A'Mighty. look yonder at that Grizzly." We followed his excited gaze into the canyon a mile or more beneath us, and we saw the gleam of his grey back as he lumbered off out of sight in the timber. We were spell-bound; and again the big brute came out into a clearing still further ahead; but no dogs were in sight, or men to put them on the trail.

I said, "Dad gum the luck, I believe he is going to get clean away, where in thunder are all the dogs anyhow; let's see if we can make it around the heads of these canyons to the other side of Limpia in time to get a shot at him as he tops out." We rode as fast as our horses could keep their footing over these rock-slides and sleek carpet of pine-needles, but the odds were all against us; as the big bear had already crossed over and taken his plunge into the wilds of Merrill Canyon, or some of its many tributaries. Not a dog, nor a yelp of a dog; we were in a frenzy of keen disappointment, as a bear like this monster had never been seen in all of our hunting in the Davis Mountains; and to let him get away, it was tough luck.

At the beginning of the excitement in Briggs Spring Gap, it developed that the dogs were after several different kinds of varmints and did not get any of them.

My father, G. W. Evans, the oldest bear hunter in this country, topped out with some of the boys further east on Livermore than I did, and he had gathered up several of the dogs that had gotten away. He came to a point overlooking Limpia when the dogs began to act strangely; their hair was standing on end, and with their tails tucked under them, they came back to the man and got close under the horses, as if they were scared to death. Presently the hunters came to a wide swath cut in the under-brush, bushes broken down, or pulled up by the roots, and a tree pushed over. At the end of the drag was a dead cow that had been killed in the early morning that had been party devoured by some great beast, which left no track on the rock floor with only crevices, out from which sprung the mountain timber.

The old bear dogs that had trailed and treed hundreds of black bear would not trail this animal; but some of the pups carried the trail a mile or so; they all turned back except an old stray dog that did not belong to any of the outfit; the old dog followed along on the trail, barking only occasionally, while the tremendous silence in the vastness of the mountains became almost over-powering, broken only by the faint yelps of the faithful old dog.

All the while, the army of men were combing the outlying ridges, stopping, looking and listening, while hours wore on and the sun began to swing around to the west, when each one of us began to wonder where were the others, and where were all the dogs?

I was standing on a point far to the south of Livermore, several miles out from our usual hunting zone with Watt Reynolds (now deceased); we had been in this lonely place for an hour when a faint shot was heard somewhere to southeast of us, followed by a roar of some enraged animal.

Watt says, "Somebody is killing somebody's bull over there; did you ever hear such a bellow?"

There were several more shots fired in quick succession, then utter silence reigned. In the mantime, Watt and I were heading back along the "back-bone" and around the heads of the canyons in the direction from which the shots came. On our way we caught up with some more of the party who had heard the shots; when all of a sudden our horses jammed into each other; Uncle Alf Means was in the lead, and his horse, a beautiful sorrel, stepped in the crevice of a rock and snapped his foreleg completely off and left the hoof in the crevice as he rolled over; he was going at such speed when he fell, that he threw his rider clear. There was nothing we could do but put a bullet through the head of the spirited animal. Uncle Alf mounted up behind Huling Means and we went on; we knew where to go now, as there was a horn solo in the canyon ahead of us, but we had never heard this kind of a continuous serenade before in the Davis Mountains.

Making our way off down the mountain and into the dense brush in the canyon, we rounded a little cliff and came up on Uncle John Means and C. O. (Ote) Finley standing over the huge carcass of the fallen Monarch of the mountains, a Silver Tip bear; we had no scales, but he looked as big as a bull; his head was immense; while his claws, which had been bared in his death struggle, were three inches long, one inch wide, and thick as a pencil. His fur was nearly black next to the skin, while the outer half was bright silver, with a black tip on the extreme end; the fur on the legs was somewhat sandy.

The old dog had followed along, far behind the bear, and his occassional yelp, led the two hunters to the place where the bear had stopped to make his final stand. When the men got down to where the little bluff was, they dismounted and climbed up and looked over; when directly below them lay the huge bear; they both fired at the same time; the bear gave a mighty roar and charged towards them, while they began to pump 30-30 bullets into him as fast as they could work the levers.

At their first shots, the faithful old dog came a little too close to the bear, when the enraged beast made a sweep at the dog and crushed him like an egg shell. He was much more ferocious than any black bear they had ever wounded.

We who had reached the spot kept blowing our horns till a few others straggled in; but only nine men out of the twenty five who started the chase, got to see the great bear as he lay there in such terrific awesomeness, even in death.

As the shadows of the coming night heightened the gloom of the mountain fastness, we loaded the great hide with its head and feet on the largest horse we had; and it took all nine of us to handle the slippery, unwieldly burden, which we tied securely around the middle of this big horse. The rider with Mr. Ote, headed down through the rough canyon country to the Kelley ranch with their prize, where they loaded it on to a hack and headed for Rick Pile.

In the meantime, the other seven of us had to cross several deep canyons and negotiate some of the roughest and brushiest part of the Davis Mountains before we reached camp at night-fall. I had to ride on two saddles on one horse over all this tortuous course; but we brought the biggest news of the biggest bear ever killed in Texas to the excited folks in Rock Pile Camp that night.

Ote Finley kept the skin as a trophy in his ranch home for years; he mounted one of the claws as a brooch for his wife; and Uncle John and my father had gold in-laid watch fobs with these huge claws dangling from their watch chains, embelished with masonic emblems on each side.

Those were the days before the cameras had come into common usage; and the great bear was never seen by other eyes than the eyes of the men who killed him and skinned him.

Note: It is an item of unusual historical interest; that the skull of this particular bear rests in a glass case in the Smithsonian Institution, and is recorded as the only speciman of its kind known.

Linda Faulk

Panther
At Bay

TO THE GLORY OF THE POT-LICKER

To The Glory of "The Licker"

By WILL F. EVANS

From The Pioneer Magazine, San Antonio

A fine July rain had just fallen, and late at evening, as the red-oaks cast their shadows out over the hill-sides in the little horse-pasture, we take a stroll thru the brush and across the ravines, reveling in the sweet smell of it all and drinking in the pure air as it comes down to us so softly from the high mountains all about, little recking that the eyes of a beast of prey were upon our every movement.

And at sunset, when the great orb of day dropped down over the western hills, we suspected nothing sinister as we drove the four little milk-calves down into the timbered ravine and pushed them off into the water for their first drink of rain water; and tho we suspected nothing, the instinct of the calves warned them of an enemy in the brush nearby, for they seemed unduly scared of something.

But we left them there in the creek and we went back thru the milk-pens for the house; and again, just at dusk, I thought it was strange that the calves came running back to the pen, and I noticed only three of them, but as it was growing dark, I thought the other calf might be behind a dagger. And though the cows were lowing franticly, we knew it was the nature of a cow to raise a rucous on being separated from her new calf, and we thought nothing more of it.

But in the early morning as I opened the pasture gate to let in the calves, there were only three of the little fellows hanging around the pen; then the truth flashed over me at once; the reluctance of the little calves to go near the brush, their wild run back to the corrals, only the three of them; and the un-usually distressful lowing of the cows, told me the tale.

I walked straight to the timbered creek, and as I made my way down the steep incline, there, sure enough, lay the fine Hereford calf with a cruel hole eaten in its side, and the brush and leaves lying over it intact just like the great beast had left its clever work — a hasty search by the early light disclosed one round track in the creek bed — the track of a mountain lion, or panther, plenty big enough to kill a cow as well as a calf; so the sequel to this tale follows very swiftly.

We are blessed with a telephone, so the news is flashed from ranch to ranch, and horses, dogs, men, women and children were on hand by the middle of the afternoon and all were in eager anticipation.

The coyotes, the skulking scavengers that follow hard on the heels of the larger beasts of prey, to clean up the kill, were making things hideous with their howling, and the dogs were all tied fast, or the younger ones would be off chasing coyotes. The cow ponies were herded out till dark and then put in the pen for very near future use; and before daylight eleven men and boys were mounted; the young dogs were held back, and only Ring and Fly were allowed to the calf.

Yes, Ring picks up the scent, then Fly; the old panther had come back to his kill to make another meal — and now the whole pack joined in — in the prettiest music an old hunter ever heard.

To keep in hearing of these dogs on the hot trail, we trusted in the sure-footedness of our ponies and our own ability to ward off low-hanging limbs as we crossed the canyons in this wild, early morning ride. Where the ledges became thicker and the bluffs of a big canyon began to loom up over us the trail waxed hotter; and then there was a lull just at dawn; and the men began to pull their guns from their scabbards, for they knew that the old "calf-killer" had leaped out on a jutting rock somewhere and had left his trail in mid-air where old Ring couldn't pick it up — and incidently, this is a very critical moment in panther chasing, for if you prowl around too close Mr. Panther takes great leaps from cliff to cliff, and if the cliffs are high and far apart, he gets away entirely.

Three of the fellows follow along under the rim and top out, but the rest of us stay under the bluff and search its broken sides in the dim light for the hiding place of the panther.

The welcome light of dawn brings out the cliff in bold relief, and there, perched on a high pinnacle out from the main bluff, sets the panther giving her entire attention to the dogs that have just now located her, and are making frantic efforts to leap the gap and land on the narrow ledge with her.

The big panther looked to be four feet high as she stood in silhouette against the morning sky — none of us will ever forget the picture there in the early morning, and the dogs leaping about trying to get to her, and then the sharp crack of a rifle, a fusilade of bullets, and down she comes over backwards. Men, dogs and the panther all meet in the rock slides at the base of the cliff, but the guns are no longer needed, for the old panther is dead; though the excited dogs do a lot of "wooling" as they gnaw the tough hide of their fallen foe.

The sun is not up yet, as we roll the panther off down into the canyon, swing it up in front of one of the hunters and head for the ranch, all gloriously happy.

Once again, the old long-eared hounds have covered themselves with glory by sticking true to the panther trail thru a net-work of coyote tracks which were fresher than those made by the panther. The old hound is man's best friend.

Wild

SHORT-EARED DOG

Linda Faulk

The Proof of the Pudding is in the Eating

The Proof of The Pudding is in The Eating

By WILL F. EVANS

From Hunter-Trader-Trapper

Having been raised up in a "long-eared-dog-country", and knowing the "cold-nose" of the old "pot-licker" for what he is; the best trailer for beasts of prey of any dog on earth, I don't hesitate to back the old long-ears against any short-eared dog in the world.

My daddy, and his father before him, hunted coons, cats and foxes, panther, bear and leopards when all the west was wild and over-run with game, and they always trusted the unerring nose of the old dogs which never led them wrong.

One morning just about day-light, when my father was only ten years old, he shouldered his daddy's heavy old rifle, followed the old hounds on a hot trail in the dense jungle of the Colorado river "bottom"; and stepping over a drift where the dogs were at bay, he looked right into the wide-open mouth of a huge leopard; the lad pulled the trigger and nearly blowed the leopard's head off. From that day on, he and all of his sons have hunted with this strain of hounds.

Then again, we have lived on the frontier all of our lives, and have always felt safe when the old hounds were around; and felt sure when on the trail of big game, that the game would not get away. Big game by the hundreds have been brought to bay by these faithful dogs, and put out of commission by the rifles of the old frontiersmen. Many times these old dogs have been known to stay at the base of a tree, or at the mouth of a cave with a bear or panther at bay, waiting for the hunter to come with his gun and slay the beast.

At the turn of the century there lived in San Antonio our good friend, Hon. J. O. Terrill, noted for his legal mind and talented sons, and his fine Jersey herd out in West End, who was a valiant defender of the short-eared Walker dog.

One Christmas time when a lot of we cow-punchers were in San Antonio spending our money and having fun in the Alamo City, the Honorable J. O. whistled for his Walkers, and with some of his friends mounted on the bob-tailed horses, invited us on a chase for coyotes in the mesquite and prickly-pear jungles out in the pastures nearby. As we had shipped two of our old long-ears in from the ranch we kept these old dogs at heel while the Walkers were chasing everything that walked or moved, or flew. Presently our old dogs picked up a scent and gave tongue in the plaintive melody which sounded in such sharp contrast to the sharp staccato of the short-ears. Away went the Judges pack in a general direction which the wolf was supposed to have gone.

The Judge grinned his wide grin as he nodded ahead towards his fast running pack, and looked pitifully at the old dogs which were nosing along on the trail; but presently, back came the Walkers to pick up the trail which had never been lost by the Pot-lickers; then again they would tear out; and this time they jumped the wolf; and none of us had ever seen a pack of dogs run as fast as these dogs did; but each time they had to circle back and fall in with the old dogs to get the trail again. Their wild runs finally scared the wolf off into another country and he got away entirely.

Through the years we have had many hunters from the low lands enjoy our wild hunts with us; and to show their appreciation to us, when they went back home, they would sometimes send us one of their pet hunting dogs, which would invariably be of the short-eared breed, which are speedy and full of fight.

And speaking of full of fight; we can give you an allustration of the difference between fight and courage; we had one of these fightinest, runninist dogs we ever saw, till the real test came: the dogs bayed up a cat in cave near the EV ranch, and the Walker dog would not even let one of our dogs get near the cave; presently the dog made a dive into the cave and met the cat coming out; what happened then will be long remembered; the cat got a grip on the dogs lip, and we had never heard such a yelp of pain and fear as emerged from that dogs throat; finally he shook free of the cat, and he left there with his tail between his legs, howling with terror.

The cat, emboldened by his fight with the Walker came out and got what he thought was a death-grip on old John; but John shook the cat loose and closing his wide jaws on the cat's throat there really was a cat and dog fight, that was a fight.

The cat was soon finished. See the difference?

Mainly About Four-Legged Devils

NARROW OF HIP AND WIDE OF HORN, THE MEANEST BRUTE
THAT EVER WAS BORN.

By WILL F. EVANS

From Sports Afield Magazine

When the legion of devils were cast out of the man of Bibical
times and into the herd of swine that went charging into the sea,
probably these evil spirits after they had drowned the swine landed
in Mexico and entered into the herds of Mexican steers that have
been trying men's souls ever since.

Many men live and die in the cattle business and never learn
that a full-blooded Mexican steer is the pure essence of undiluted
Hell. I'll tell you the reason why. It is because the real Mexican
steer is the meekest of all animals till the proper times comes — then,
Look out, boys! That steer is a goner if you haven't got a keen legged
horse and a good rope and know how to throw it when you get there.

We have handled a lot of these sway-back, narrow ended, big-
horned bovines in these mountains where the brush is so thick in
places that the low-hanging branches inter-lock, and it is in the dense
thickets of red-oak and briars that the evil-minded scrubs hatch out
their deviltry. And to see how they can get thru this mesh with
a six foot spread of horns and not get fastened up, is a mystery
no cowboy can fathom. And the way they can go down a rough
mountainside and then back upon top in one wide swing, can best
nearly any kind of a cowboy to head them off.

I met a bunch of these docile? animals at Kent in West Texas
one time. One of my brothers and I had received a shipment of
Mexicos. We un-loaded them and were surprised at their docile
behavior as they wandered listlessly about in the stock pens; and
on the seven mile drive to the X Ranch not a steer made a move to
run off. We put the few hundred head through the gate into the
Calf Pasture for the night and not a one ever made a skitish move.
Native cattle are always tricky when you go to corral them, and
you have to be constantly on the alert not to let one break out at
a critical moment, or the whole bunch will be gone in a stampede.

But these Mexicos huddled together like sheep as they were driven thru the wide wire gate.

We had a great visit with the X boys that night and turned in at a late hour, expecting to round up the steers and get them out of the holding pasture by sun-up probably, to get an early start on the 25 mile drive to the Nunn Ranch. The cook called us to breakfast while it was still inky black dark, but we thought nothing of that. We only congratulated ourselves on being able to get such an early start with our steers.

MEXICAN STEER

Linda Faulk.

And just because it is called the Calf Pasture, don't you imagine that it is a little alfalfa field of 30 acres. No sir! It covers a couple of sections of foot hills that are several hundred feet high, and so rough in places that a billy goat would break his neck if he didn't walk nimble. But we were not worrying about the roughness of the pasture, as we were accustomed to working in rough country.

It developed that the inky blackness was caused by a dense fog which lasted two days and nights; in the meantime our supposedly gentle Mexicos had topped out and "located" in the very roughest parts of the mountainous pasture. And when we started the drive with the help of some of the X boys we found out something about Mexican steers that we will never forget. Those steers had no intentions whatever of coming out of those roughs — when we would start a bunch off down a mountain they would run like deer and circle back on top of the ridge again: we ran our horses down in trying to get them off, and still there were some which would get away, and part of them jumped the fence into Gomez Pasture; and it took a long time to get them back. While I was making a determined effort to head off a bunch to keep them from circling back on top again, while running at great speed, my wonderful cutting horse, "Jim" snapped a leader in his front leg low down; and only the Grace of God, and the best piece of horse flesh ever trusted into a man's keeping, saved me from a terrible tragedy, for the great horse kept his balance on his three good legs and did not turn over down the mountain with me.

I un-saddled him as he stood there, quivering with the pain; and from that day on I have hated a Mexican steer — for they verified their hellish natures in hundreds of ways as long as we owned them and tried to get them out of the roughs and the dense thickets where they took up their habitat on the Nunn Ranch. They would not stay in open country, but always hid out where it was hard to find them and next to impossible to get them out; and we had to shoot many of them, butcher them on the spot and carry them out on pack horses. The cowboy knows no such word as fail in his line of business. We won out in handling Mexican steers; but never again, in a rough, brushy country.

WHERE THE WORLD EDGES OFF

Where The World Edges Off

A THRILLING TRIP IN A WILD AND DESOLATE REGION.

By WILL F. EVANS

From Sports Afield Magazine

The great basin of the Rio Grande from the Eagle Mountains south of Sierra Blanca to the Chinati Mountains southwest of Marfa, Texas, holds a weird fascination peculiary its own. When you feel its awful desolation get a grip on you, you want to flee back to your own kind of civilization; but when you have left this painted desert of loneliness and lofty rim-rocks, the call of the wild keeps gently knocking upon the door of your primitive nature; and if you would heed the call, you would take your pack outfit and go jogging along down amongst the gray, forbodding hills again.

Our car, a big Nash, went bowling along over the broad prairies and rolling hills as we left Valentine headed for the Rio Grande towards the famous Hereford ranch of Luke Brite, where the tobosa changed to gramma, and the mountains began to hedge us in from all sides. We had been gradually going up grade till we were up nearly 5,000 feet while still on the prairie, which we soon left as we began to climb the rough hills; when we made a sudden turn down a rock gorge, made a few sharp curves going upward in low gear, and we were on the noted Rim Rock looking off into space — just a few steps from the car, and we were gazing off into another world — a panorma terrific in its awsome splendor of painted, barren hills, sharp and jagged peaks, deep, and crooked canyons — an air-plane view from our exalted perch on old terra firma; which to the "tender-foot", might look inviting for a hike, but from the old cow-man's eyes, the treacherous land down under was clothed with millions of thorny cacti, and walled in by impassable barriers to block the way if on horse-back, and a dangerous footing when walking.

Black cliffs tower upwards over us as we slip through the only gap that nature has left in the rim-rock along here; our driver starts down in low gear taking the fearful descent around the horse-shoe curves and hair-pin twists down the famous Candelaria Hill. Down, down, down we go, into Capote creek, splashing in the clear waters of the mountain stream, while sharp pinnacles stick up like hugh fingers on each side of us.

Soon the pungent smell of the cachanillo, a rank weed of the river bottoms, tickles the nostrils, and we know we are nearing the river, while the willows tornillos, thorny under-brush and giant cotton-woods begin to hedge us in as we negotiate the fastness of this jungle-land. Looking backwards we see the huge Rim Rock standing like a great wall, still looming upwards, tho many miles away. We skirt the bank of the muddy old stream which separates our land from the land of the tamale and the burro — the land of to-morrow, where to-day is of supreme importance and the future is a long, long way off. It is restful and soothing to the frayed nerves of the Gringo to mingle with the pleasure-loving, music-loving people who are our good neighbors across the way — it gives us another slant on life which is good for our peace of mind.

The river zig-zags back and forth across the wide valley; within each bend lies fertile soil very productive when cleared of its jungle — and many farms of cotton, alfalfa and garden, especially corn and frijoles are irrigated from ditches taken out far up the river from the most primative dams: the out-bends of the river are invariably walled in by the gray, thorn-clad hills or lime-stone bluffs; and many times the primitive road and the ancient ditches are carved out of the same hillside and go winding along together: one ancient ditch crossed under our road many times in a distance of a few miles — old mesquite trees along this ditch sprung up as seedlings long after the ditch had been built with forked sticks and burros.

At Ruidosa, 12 miles below Candelaria, the little Mexican town thru which we had just passed, we filled up with 30 cent gasoline; while only 35 miles away, at Marfa, gas was only 24 cents; but when you see the road they have to truck it over, you would think 40 cents would never be nearer the right price.

It was here at Ruidosa that Uncle Sam kept a body of soldiers to stand guard along the Border when Pancho Villa was on the warpath. We took the back track aways, then hit the Marfa road, with its many ups and down; sometimes going over the sand and gravel in the bed of an arroyo, or taking a sharp climb, then a run along a "hog-back", when suddenly the driver turned sharp to the left and scooted off to a stop in a deep canyon at famous Ruidosa Hot Springs where a hot stream of mineral water comes gushing out of the mountainside. Where a group of cabins cluster about the main bath house — where rheumatics come from all over the country — and where more booze is boiled out of drunk bums than any place along the border. The water is about the same temperature as of Marlin, Texas, but not so highly mineralized.

The road from this famous health resort leads always up and up as we get higher — and every backwards glance shows the great basin of the river to be far beneath us now.

Anon we reach the edge of Pinto Canyon and gaze across in rapture at the lofty Chinati Mountains ribbed with tier after tier of rim-rocks and belts of scrub timber: tho the scenery is sublime, and the backwards view into the great Rio Grande basin is a scene never to be forgotten, there is still no Davis Mountain turf and Davis Mountain gramma grass in evidence. The long descent into Pinto Canyon was a continuation of curves and a narrow road-way carved out of solid stone along the mountain side till we reached the bottom of the canyon.

When we leave the canyon and start to climb out over this narrow road-way, as the old car is steaming and puffing away, we are holding our breaths for fear that we might meet a freighting wagon coming down to meet us. However, our good angel was with us that day, for when we finally pulled out on top of that awful hill, a freighting wagon, heavily loaded, with a ten-burro team was parked by the roadside with just enough room for our jalopy to pass. The old Mexican driver must have heard the groaning of our laboring car as we were making the climb, and he knew better than to start down till we cleared the road. From a chorus of muncha gracious from all five of us, the old man learned that we were deeply appreciative of his waiting for us to come out.

We are now on the great divide in the gramma grass belt, where the land dips to the east and the waters drain into the Pecos River; we have left one "world" of another kind and of another elevation and have topped out onto the Highlands.

"In The Grip of A Texas Blizzard"

A "BLUE" NORTHER DEALS REAL MISERY TO A COW PUNCHER WHEN HE IS UN-PREPARED FOR IT.

By WILL F. EVANS

From The Pioneer, San Antonio, Texas

The trouble all started when I bought a bunch of real Texas cattle from a Mexican down under the Rim near Shafter; but the main trouble was, when I agreed with the old man to have his Vaqueros deliver the cattle to me in the stock-pens at Marfa.

Gavino's ranch was in the gray, forbidding foot-hills which were cut up by hundreds of ravines, both deep and shallow, but nearly all of them difficult to cross on horse-back.

From the crest of the thorn-covered ridges we, could gaze across the Rio Concho and could see the hills and mountains jutting up from the valleys in Old Mexico; we could see the river glistening in the sun-light far away, as it meandered along towards it union with the Rio Grande; and could see the dim out-lines of the adobe village of Ojinaga, the famous Mexican town, the oldest and quaintest settlement between El Paso and San Antonio.

If you ever buy a bunch of cattle from a Mexican in the Rio Grande region, go get 'em yourself, with your own cowboys; pay for the cattle at the ranch and drive them to your destination with your own trusted men. (Note: In those days the big cattle trucks had not come into service, and cattle had to be driven overland, ragardless of terrain or distance).

I made my way back to the EV ranch, a hundred miles from Gavino's, having agreed to receive the 250 head as soon as Gavino's Peons could gather them and drive them up there.

And thereby hangs a tale; speaking of tails, the Mexican Vaquero is an adept at leaning off, grabbing the tail of a fleeing cow or steer, and with the swift wrapping of the end of the tail around the saddle-horn, turns sharply off at right angles and throws the hapless brute a terrific fall: and a lot of this surely happened to my cattle which were fat and sleek when I bought them.

The cattle must evidently had been held in corrals from the

start of the "work" till the last cow was gathered; for when I took a look at them in the stock-pens at Marfa, I almost had heart failure. It was nearly night-fall; there was no water in the troughs in the stock-pens, and the Agent would not turn the water on unless the cattle were billed for shipment over his road; we did not have time to drive them several miles to a ranch to water them; and they were too near dead to have made the trip anyway: if it had not been for an accommodating High Official of the Railroad, who overheard my argument with the Agent, those cattle would have litterally starved to death on me for lack of water that night. After the cattle had drank their fill we moved them out of the stock-pens and headed for the Smith Bros. Ranch a few miles out; but the poor brutes were so weak that their hind legs wrapped around each other when they walked (any old cowman knows what that means to a cow) ; and when we drove them thru the gate to pass them thru W. A. Mimms' calf pasture with its knee-high gramma grass, the hungry cattle litterally buried their noses in the tall grass, and we could not budge them a foot.

Mr. Mimms was a real western man with a western man's big heart and understanding.

I had never seen him, nor he had never seen me, but when I told him who I was, and what I was up against, he said; "I know your daddy well, and George Evans' boys are welcome to anything I have." He not only let us use his little pasture for our cattle and our horses, but he let us camp in his barn-yard and furnished us wood for our camp-fire.

We moved the cattle out early, on our way to Smith Brothers, our first ranch along the way; but the sun failed to give any warmth, and the slanting rays looked very blue; but still we did not know that we were about to face one of the most dreaded of all phenomenons, the Texas Blizzard. It was only a few short miles up the draws to Smith Bros. ranch, where there were friends, shelter and pasturage for our cattle; but the hungry, sore-footed cattle failed to cover that distance: the facts were staring us in the face, that we three boys and the Mexican wagon-driver were going to have to stand guard around these cattle in the "jaws" of a blizzard; the thought was really terrifying.

Our hands were already freezing to the bridle-reins, and by the time we got the cattle headed for a cove in the bluffs near the road, the ice-laden wind from the north was howling like furies.

The cattle began to mill with the eddying gusts, churning up gravel that hit us in the face. If it had not been for the Mexican's ability to light a fire in a gale, we would probably gone without supper and breakfast. This hombre curled himself around a little pile of wood and kindling and soon had the fire flaming; but the Mexican kid could not cook, so that job fell to me; but the wind whipped the flour out of the pan, blowed the coals out from under skillet and off of the lid, when I did finally dump the dough in.

That night will stand out in my memory as the most miserable night in all my life. The cattle moaned with the wind as they milled constantly all night long. Some of the cows' feet were frozen, and one yearlin froze to death in the piercing cold.

The water troughs at Smith Brothers' were frozen solid; and at high noon at the Oscar Medley ranch, we had to chop out ice with an axe, and found very little water in the bottom of troughs near the center. We turned our little herd into the holding pasture at the Gillett Barrel Springs Ranch for the night. The warm hearts and the warm homes of our friends along the way more than balances the account against our sufferings from the cold in the blizzard.

He Had "Rollers" In His Nose

THIS KIND OF A SNORT IS USUALLY A COMBINATION OF FEAR AND BRAVADO IN A HORSE.

By WILL F. EVANS

From El Paso Live Stock Journal

We have, all of us, at some times in our lives, been almost lifted out of our seats by the great nasal explosion from some old Roman-nosed, he-man who blows his nose like a jack-ass a braying, or a combination of heavy thunder and the screech of air-brakes. But when you see this propinquity fully developed in a horse, and hear him perform as he runs backwards on the rope, and shows you the whites of his eyes, he must feel like the nigger in the song; "Nobody know how bad ah is."

We had one of those "bad" horses, a blood-bay, that we called "Mexican"; he had those "rollers" developed to a startling degree; in fact he could make the most ferocious snorting of any I ever heard; he could really scare you.

Most horses which snort and roll their eyes, and act bad general-ly, wont buck; but "Mexican" was different; he would buck you off at the slighest warning; and it was dangerous to get near his heels.

We were camped at Rock Pile in the days of the open range, when my father was running the wagon; father had the bay snorter along, but he just rode him when he had to, as it took so long to bridle the out-law and saddle him; and Mexican began to get fat; meaner than ever. One day he traded Mexican to John Cole, his "Straw Boss", for a gentler horse. John and a bunch of the boys were dis-patched to move a bunch of cattle to another part of the range — I was a small kid then; tho I was a good cow hand; and I went along to help drive the cattle.

Along in mid-afternoon a huge covy of blue quail attracted the boys attention, when several of them jumped off and began to throw rocks at the quail, thinking they might kill a few of these lucious birds for supper. The quail refused to fly, but kept dodging around thru the willows — John had to join in; but every time he would raise his hand to throw, Mexican would run backwards and snort, and make John miss his quail — then John tied his rope in the bridle reins and proceeded to throw some more rocks; but still the horse would jirk backwards and make John lose his aim.

All the while John was getting madder and madder; in this mad rage he managed to climb into the saddle while Mexican was doing everything in his power to keep the man from mounting.

We really had a wild west scene in action now — all the boys stopped throwing at quail and watched the performance: but about the third jump Mexican threw John high in the air, John came down cènter over the saddle-horn, his big paunch folded over the horn, and John's body whirled like a windmill as he went round and around, grabbing off the bridle as he was thrown into a huge bundle in the brush.

Mexican, the real bad horse, was a bad horse on the run now, with the rope still tied in the bridles reins which John was clutching — he was a madder, but much meeker man, now.

It took so long to run the horse down and rope him, that we did not get back to camp till after dar k.   Father was furious and wanted to know what had kept us so long; and one of the boys said, "We had a hell of a time roping Johnnie's out-law horse.

Of course it had to be explained how the horse got loose, etc. — Johnnie was finally pinned down and owned up that the horse had pitched him off — but Johnnie said too much — that he was just riding along, and the horse had him thrown off before he knew what happened. I was dumbfounded by Johnnie's reply, and was mad because the boys, who had witnessed the whole thing, let Johnnie get away with it; so I blurted out the facts — Johnnie had mounted the horse to "take it out of him", and had given the horse a "rowling" that no horse would take, especially one with the evil temper of Mexican.   All the boys, except Johnnie, patted me on the back, and roared with laughter.

Rube on UN GREY

Linda Faulk

Raining Grindstones, Pitchforks and Pitching Horses

A DRAMA IN REAL LIFE WITH AN AUDIENCE OF ONE LONE COWBOY.

By WILL F. EVANS

From El Paso Live Stock Journal

Anything can, and does happen to a cow-puncher, especially in Texas, which is a great old State; it is so broad and so long, that West Texas raises up one class of people, while East Texas raises up another class, entirely different: North Texas produces Oil Magnates, while South Texas raises Negroes, rice and bananas and the old-time Southern gentleman.

And speaking of rain; West Texas can deliver the "Wet Stuff" when she takes a notion. To lead up to my story; friend Jess Fisher, traded for a small gray horse with an evil eye, the movements of a panther and the makings of a real mountain climbing horse.

This horse had the reputation of always throwing his rider when he did pitch; but having the instinct that he could not get Jess out of the saddle, he never tried it. Jess gave the horse to Rube because he was such a sure-footed horse in the roughs. The horse had a suspicion that Rube would be pretty hard to dis-lodge from the saddle also, so he continued in his meek role, biding his time, which came with the suddenness of the cloud-burst which engulfed Rube and I as we were out riding the range.

There was a drought on, and we were thinking " 'Taint gonna rain no mo," as there wasn' a cloud in sight anywhere: but we reckoned without the vicissitudes of West Texas weather; and of course we were in our shirt sleeves, with only our leggin's to protect us from the brush. We had gotten to the far side of the range, when the clouds began to pile up, one above the other and bulge out at the bottom, when the whole bottom seemed to fall out; we raced for a wide-spreading oak to keep from drowning; tho we were already drenched to the bone; the wind whipped the sheets of water against us from all sides; the cold air was very piercing; the lighting flashes and the roaring thunder came at the same instant; we were really seeing the raw elements of nature performing in wildest grandeur.

There was a rift in the black cloud over-head, and a sudden calm in the midst of the storm; so Rube said, "We had better pull for the ranch, or we can't ever get up the old creek". (Note: Cherry Canyon, on the upper tributaries of which, the Nunn Ranch is located, has to be crossed many times; and as it is walled in with high bluffs on each side in places, the only way it can be negotiated is up the canyon's bed.) So we decided that we should lose no time in reaching headquarters; but we were not prepared for what was going to happen as swift and sudden as the Cloud-burst did.

When Rube gripped the saddle-horn and left the ground, all the chained devils in that grey horse, broke forth with all their fury; no stunt that I have ever seen pulled off in any wild West Rodeo equaled the mad pitching of that grey demon in that storm; he pitched forewards, backwards, sun-fished, and tried all of his bag of tricks; but finally quit from exhaustion.

I was as glad as Rube was, when this terrific bucking ceased, as I could have never roped this fleet pony on the large old sorrel Millican horse I was riding; and he certainly gave Rube a shaking up which left him weak for several days.

(70)

"Twas on One Sunday Morn"

BUT THE TWO COWBOYS TACKLED SOMETHING WORSE THAN A BEAR.

By WILL F. EVANS

From The Pioneer, San Antonio, Texas

Perhaps we have most of us heard the rollicking song of the "Preacher and the Bear".

Rube and Ell did not meet any Grizzly on that particular Sunday morning; in fact, they did not meet anything, but they came in close personal contact with something as wild and as vicous as a Grizzly.

Responsibilities pertaining to ranch work are usually forgotten on Sunday; and when the round-up is not on, the cowboys take it easy by doing nothing at all but killing time. Like the old lady who had to work 16 hours a day the most of her life, when she got a chance to rest, she "jest set"; so some of the boys amused themselves by following the old lady's formula; but the two young Evans boys had too much energy to ever sit still.

They spent a lot of this energy that morning in saddling two wild broncs, which they had to blind-fold to saddle and mount; when they lifted the blinds, they yelled to the by-standers, "open the gate and let 'em out"; and they were gone down the canyon in a wild run, matching their own energy against that of the colts.

There is a rough, brushy canyon on the Nunn Ranch, called "Bicycle, so named because Uncle John Means lost a horse by that name, which had dis-appeared for several months, when one day the horse was found in this canyon; and it has worn the name of Bicycle ever since. And the horse is not the only animal which has hidden out and staid hidden; for it has sheltered out-law cattle for half a century. There was a roan Mexico steer which had not been seen for several months; and he was one of the very wildest and most vicious one of our bunch of Mexicos — and as luck would have it; or ill-luck, if you wish; these boys, on their wild mounts, not even bridle-wise, saw the roan steer at a distance; and the same thought gripped their young minds; to rope and tie the wild out-law on wild broncs.

(71)

Their ambition out-weighed their common sense. They managed to reach down and draw the cinches tight; took their ropes down and started the chase. The colts were racing stock, and had more speed than the long-legged steer. Rube nearly got a throw at the steer before the steer reached the top of the mountain; but the steer turned over the rim and shot like a rocket down the hill but Rube's bronc was so fleet, and his racing blood was so keen that he put Rube right up by the side of the steer — then a quick whirl of the loop and the steer and the pony were tied to the same rope. Then what happened next was sort of a night-mare to Rube — the steer was heavier than the horse; the horse was jerked down and Rube was "knocked out"; when he came to, his foot was hung in a stirrup, the horse was kicking at him, and the steer was reaching for him with his long horns. Rube was yelling to Ell, who was trying to get his un-managible bronc near the fracas, to, "Keep the steer off of me, keep the steer off of me."

When Ell finally succeeded in roping the steer, the un-usual weight of the steer and Rube's running horse, pulled Ell's saddle to one side, then his horse began to buck. There was a bucking horse on each end of the ropes and a steer in the middle, while Rube was fastened to his saddle that wa s hung under his horse's belly.

For awhile it looked as if Rube would either be dragged or kicked to death, or gored by the steer, as Ell was doing his best to keep his seat on his own horse which was trying to buck him off everytime he got near the steer.

These reckless boys not only tied the roan out-law — they brought him into the pens at the ends of their ropes — and he was the maddest steer I have ever seen. The only way the boys could keep the steer from goring their horses was for one of them to lead out, and the other stay in the rear, thus keeping the mad steer on a tight line between them.

He was foaming at the mouth, and would run at the fence and try to knock it down as we were sitting on the high rails looking at him. This was one Sunday morn which will stay in their memory as long as these two boys live.

John J. Means sitting on
Dead black bear.

Bear Knowledge

By JOE M. EVANS
From his book: "A Corral Full of Stories"

I was raised on a horse, and began hunting as soon as I could reach the trigger on a short saddle-rifle. One of the first things I can remember was following a pack of dogs and my father after a bear in the Davis Mountains; and just as soon I got big enough to hold the gun to my shoulder, my father would let me shoot the bear up in a tree. It was always close range, and a big target, easy to hit. I had good luck the first few times and got to where I didn't think I could miss one.

When I got a little older, some hunters from El Paso, Floyd Payne and Mr. Shelton, gave me a 38 caliber carbine. By that time I had begun to run off and leave my father in the rough mountains when the dogs got after a bear. This experience led me to believe that there wasn't anybody that could beat me to a bear. I had good horses, knew the trails in the mountains, and knew how to get up and down the canyons. I also knew the dogs and loved them and they loved me. If you have never seen a boy and a horse and dog together, you don't know anything about real happiness.

Of all the thrills that can come to a boy, it is thru this combination. Then turn him loose in the mountains where there are bear, mountain lions and all kinds of wild animals; if he doesn't get killed, he is sure to have the greatest time that is possible for a boy to have.

After I had had several years of this thrilling excitement and had killed a number of bear, I began to challange the real, old bear hunters. I had an uncle whom I thought a lot of, and I had heard my father say many times what a great hunter my uncle was. I had never hunted with him, but was very anxious to do so, just to show him how little he knew about hunting bear.

It was at a round up that I saw my uncle after he had been working cattle for almost a month without a shave. He was about 40 years old and had some grey hair in his black beard. I'll never forget when I challenged him for this bear hunt. I said to him, "Uncle John we are going to pull off a bear hunt over in the mountains next week. Come over and I will show you how to kill a bear." He stopped his horse dead still and leaned over to one side in his

(74)

saddle and began rubbing his chin and said to me, "Joe, you see this frost on my chin? That's all bear knowledge. Every grey hair there represents a bear race and experience hunting bear." I said to him, "You'll need all the experience and knowledge and training you can muster up if you beat me to a bear."

There were plenty of bear in those days and we had a good pack of dogs, all kinds of good saddle horses, and not much to do but hunt. Everything was all set for my uncle John Means, to come over to our ranch in the Davis Mountains for the hunt. We shod up our good horses, had the dogs all in fine shape and everything ready for the big time. My uncle and his son Sam, came in a buggy working two horses, one a big sorrel called Ed. Old Ed had a big foot, and was a work-horse besides. Something we seldom ever did was to ride anything except a real cow pony in the mountains after a wild cattle or on a bear hunt, because it takes a good horse to catch either.

I had a good horse shod and ready for Uncle John, but he insisted on riding Old Ed. I argued with him and tried to persuade him to ride a good horse, because I didn't want to take advantage of him, since he would need the best horse he could find if he stood any chance with me when we got after a bear.

We got up next morning long before daylight and loosed the dogs and started out as soon as it was light enough to see. Uncle John rode old Ed, his old work-horse. We hadn't gone far from camp until the dogs struck a hot bear-trail and left there like lightning. I said to my cousin, Sam Means, a boy just about my age, "Come on Sam, stay with me if you want to kill the bear," and off we started. You talk about tearing down the brush and running over rocks and anything else that got in our way; we did not pay any attention to anything, but were trying to stay up with the dogs. They went straight up a high mountain; it began to get steeper and rougher, and the dogs were getting further away; finally we ran our horses down, and had to stop to let them catch their wind.

From where we stopped we heard the dogs run back down the mountain. We didn't lose any time but headed down the mountain as fast as our horses could run. I was in the lead and going full speed when I came to a big Juniper tree. I was all set to go to the right of the tree and the horse had decided to go to the left, so we landed right in the middle of the tree. The tree had big, spreading branches and my horse lodged in the fork of one, and there I was, fastened in the fork of the Juniper tree.

We finally got the horse out by taking the saddle off and pulling him over backwards. All of this took considerable time. Just about the time we were saddled up and ready to go again we heard the dogs treed; and in a few minutes we heard a rifle shot. We rode on down into the bottom of the canyon where we had heard the dogs and the shot, and there was my uncle John sitting on a big black bear, holding his gun in one hand and rubbing his chin with the other. I didn't say much, neither did Sam. We were very much humiliated. I finally got up enough courage to say, "Well, let's clean him and hang him up in one of these trees in a cool place. We'll get another one; it's early yet."

The sun was just coming up over the mountains and we went on hunting; and sure enough, we did get after another bear. I said to Sam, "This time you go up the ridge and I'll follow the dogs, and we will have two chances at him." The dogs treed this bear in a big tree on top of a mountain so rough it was impossible to ride anywhere close to the tree. I could see the bear go up this tall pine and stay awhile, then come down to where the dogs could reach him; then the grand fight would come off. The dogs would bite him on his hind legs, which is something a bear can't stand, for this seems to be his tender spot. After one of these fights he would climb to the top of the tree licking his hind legs where the dogs had bitten him.

I was climbing up the steep mountain in sight of the bear while all of this was happening. Just before I got close enough to kill him, he came down and another big fight took place. But this time he didn't go back up the tree but went out over the mountain exactly in the opposite direction from where I was.

My horse was a mile back down the mountain side, so the only thing left for me to do was to scramble back down the mountain, get my horse and start all over again. I had a long ride to make to get around this big mountain and I rode as fast as it was possible thru the brush and over the boulders. I finally hit a trail leading up to the canyon and could make faster time. After I had gone a short distance on the trail I noticed a horse track. You remember my telling you at the beginning of this story of my uncle John riding "Old Ed", a big-footed old work horse. This horse track in the trail was without question, Old Ed's track. I knew without any doubt that uncle John was ahead of me, and this simply made me sick; but I kept on going in the direction where I had last heard the dogs. I rode out on a high point to listen, and I heard the dogs.

While I was trying to figure out the best route to get to them, crack went a rifle shot. This made me still sicker. I was in hopes it was Sam, who fired the shot; but my better judgment told me, from the horse track I had seen in the trail, that it was uncle John's rifle I had heard. There was nothing left to do but to get over there and find out. When I reached the spot there sat uncle John on another big black bear, rubbing his chin. About that time Sam rode up from another direction. His horse was like mine, wet with sweat, and almost run to death; I had lost my hat and had torn my shirt and skinned my face running thru the brush. Uncle John had killed this bear without any effort or without striking a gallop. Old Ed was as fresh as if he had just been saddled up; as uncle John had taken plenty of time to pick his way thru the brush and hadn't gotten a scratch. He sat there rubbing his chin, and called our attention to his "Bear Knowledge" by remarking, "Every grey hair on my chin represents, bear knowledge."

Linda Faulk.

OLD BROWNIE
(Texas)

Davis Mountains Brownie West Texas' Most Famous Bear Dog

By WILL F. EVANS

From Sports Afield Magazine

Situated in one of the most picturesque short canyons in West Texas, is the Evans ranch, which had three Perkins wind-mills lined up across the canyon; large stock corrals built out of split railroad ties when the long-horn cattle and long-eared hounds mingled with the many children which were raised up in this wild gorge.

One of the old-timers of El Paso, W. F. Payne, once sent my father a very small, scraggy looking brown pup in the days of big game and the good old times of the open-range days. This was Brownie, mild of manner and devoid of the rapacious qualities that characterize most dogs.

When he was six month old, in company with his mate, Bell, they would run rabbits all day, and tho not gifted with speed, these pups had the cold nose and the staying qualities; so they always brought in the rabbits for supper.

They began to forget rabbits after we had caught a few foxes and cats with them; and after they had been in at the death of a few panthers they were right up with the ring leaders of the big pack of hounds, and would disdain to even notice a rabbit after that.

When Brownie was a yearling he was at the killing of his first bear, and nothing else but the smell of a bear ever appealed to him again. For 12 years he was used as a great pilot of our pack of bear dogs. When Brownie put his nose to the ground, and then lifting one foot, with his nose pointed upward, gave forth his challenge to Bruin in pure clarion tones, the other dogs would go wild and would be off with a mighty chorus of yelps. No stopping them then! The great leader of Dogdom had given the command, and they knew he was infallible. It was up to them to catch the bear and put him up a tree, and it was up to the riders to risk their lives over the roughest, the most densely timbered, and highest mountains in Texas in their efforts to get to the three in time to kill the bear.

Leaving at daylight, or before even the faintest light appears in the east, the hunters ride out beneath the stars in the crisp morning air, everybody with a gun in his scabbard, their horses all humped up ready to buck, with old Brownie in the lead of the whole layout — all the rest of the pack being kept behind with many smothered admonitions. Occassionally a well aimed chunk will land broadside across the ribs of some smarty dog that breaks ranks, and he gives a startled yelp and slinks back in line.

About 'the time the sun casts the first blue haze across the canyons we have reached the edge of the real bear country, and as it is folly to try to follow in the direct wake of a fleshing bear — for he picks the most inaccessable country to make his get-away — Bruin must be out-witted by the hunters — and the men do this by topping out and waiting at the most strategetical passes through which the bear might come before taking his swift descent into the next canyon. The bear many times out-wits both dogs and hunters, and the poorer the bear, the further he can run, till finally the dogs are all hot and sore-footed and the horses all given out. It is then that the dogs are called off.

Before the chase is started again, we call a halt and Joe and Sam, or Jess and Edwin, will follow Brownie into another stronghold for bear with the rest of the pack at their heels. All the rest of the hunters are to watch different gaps thru which the bear might pass if he topped out, and they are advised to ride like the devil, for if you don't get there in time, and the bear has already gone thru and has a down-hill run, he will usually get away; for no animal in the world can beat a scared bear going down hill. He just falls off of anything, and if he doesn't alight on his feet it does not matter, as he curls up and rolls like a ball till he gets on his feet; then he is gone again, making every possible use of gravity in his mad flight.

At night around the camp fires, when all the other dogs are scattered around amongst the bushes cuddled up asleep, or licking their sore, bleeding paws, Brownie was usually lying down at the feet of one of the hunters — as he understood the word bear, and that was the main topic of conversation, and as Brownie was always the Star Actor in all the Plays, the constant use of his name caused him to feel like he belonged to the men's crowd.

Brownie had such a great infatuation for trailing bear, that between hunts he would leave the ranch, and would put a bear up a tree by himself. There the faithful old fellow would stay — some times for 24 hours before one of us could find him in the vast region of mesa, peaks and canyons, and kill the bear.

Brownie was never quarrelsome or greedy like most dogs, and was never known to growl at a child, altho there were always a number of children around, imposing on the dog's good nature.

After he got to be 14 years old, and could no longer be the first one to the tree, the proud old dog, after he had picked up the trail and given the signal to charge, would fall back to the horses' heels and follow Joe or my father. He nearly always got there in time to give the dead bear a shaking as he sunk his teeth into the soft fur that smelled better to him than anything else in the world.

When he was old and feeble he followed Joe and Lee out one Sunday morning into some rough country where they had gone cow hunting and found where a panther had killed a calf. Neither of them had a gun, but Brownie followed the trail for four hours over a country so broken and rock bound that Joe had to go on foot and help the feeble old dog up the bad places, while Lee took the horses and watched the gaps with the hopes of getting a chance to rope the panther. After a long time Brownie put the panther on a rock and the boys managed to get their ropes on him, and after he whirled and pitched till he was exhausted they finally stretched him out and cut his throat with the pocket knives.

A short time after this hunt Brownie died — having remained faithful and true to the last and sincerely mourned by all the bear hunters of Western Texas. He had been in at the killing of 200 bears.

(The strain of this wonderful old dog has been carried down thru the packs of Evans childrens' dogs for half a century; and many of them have been great dogs).

A Panther Hunt

SLAYING A GOAT KILLER

By WILL F. EVANS

From The Big Bend Sentinel

The pioneer blood runs strong in the veins of the sons and the grand-sons of the old timers who first glimpsed the stately grandeur of the Davis Mountains in the early Eighties as their little herds of stock and their ox-drawn wagons moved slowly along up 'Dobe Canyon. The great springs of pure water that gushed forth from the mountain's base had just been claimed by other hardy souls and were being retained "by right of possession"; but they have passed through many hands, including Winny & Finn; Gomez Cattle Co., and Newman Bros; and since 1895 have been owned by The Reynolds Cattle Co., of Fort Worth; known now as the Long X headquarter Ranch and the X orchard.

This is one of the famous beauty spots of the State because of the wonderful back-ground of majestic mountains rimmed by lofty cliffs and clothed with virgin grasses, dotted with scattering trees, lovely groves, and heavy timber. Newman Bros. branded MF on their she stuff and TN on their steers; some of the steers began to climb the high mountains to the east, and finding permanent water on the high mesas in rock cisterns, and virgin grasses, they became "located" and as wild as the deer that roamed in the roughs.

Up near the clouds in this unbelievably wild setting, stands a goat herder's camp where the sure-footed goats are brought in at night by a nimble-footed Mexican named Geronimo Segura, who has been known to reach a bayed-up panther or bear on his own nimble feet almost as soon as the dogs themselves have reached the spot.

A few days ago a panther got into his goat herd at night and killed eight goats, and then in diabolical glee killed a faithful burro; the news was carried to Will Reynolds, manager of the X Ranch; a cowboy was dispatched to the E V Ranch the home of the old long-eared hounds, where the Evans children, grand-children and great-grand-children have annual get-together meetings, and where the faithful 30-30's are always ready for the next hunt. Here the messenger found Paul and Paul, Jr., Graves and Truett.

The dogs were loaded into a special trailer and the boys started out at 3 A. M. for the X Ranch where Will and John Reynolds and Bill Cowden were waiting for them. The fat cow-ponies had been kept in the corrals overnight, and by day-light the hunters with dogs at heel were riding out into the cold morning air through the dense timber of Haw Thicket, up the steep mountain sides and onto TN Ridge to the scene of the massacre, but the panther had not returned to the kill.

Short gorges break back into the mesa walled in by rim-rocks hundreds of feet high; heavy under-brush and piled up boulders makes riding impossible at times, so the boys were on foot when the dogs struck a trail, and were scattered along for a mile or more on the rim when Paul and Paul, Jr., saw the panther in the brush far below with the dogs in close pursuit; Paul shot and knocked the panther down, but he got up and dis-appeared in the timber. Graves and Bill got a shot at it and so did the other boys, but everybody missed; the dogs were now so close to the wounded panther that they ran him into a cave. Geronimo was under the Rim on a horse, which was very unusual for him, but he had been riding far and wide trying to gather up his goats after they had scattered in all directions from the panther's attack, so he dismounted and made his way to the cave and found it to be straight down, and could see no bottom; the boys all scampered down thru the rocks and reached the place where the dogs were baying. They made a torch out of grass and paper tied on a stick and let Geronimo down in the hole on a rope with the torch in his hand; when he had gotten down about 30 feet the wounded panther gave a roar and Geronimo yelled, "geeme peestol, geeme peestol"; they hastily tied a pistol onto an-other rope and let it down to the Mexican in his very dangerous position and he shot the panther by the light of his torch.

He climbed in on the ledge by the dead panther and put a rope on its neck; the boys pulled the panther out, and then pulled the Mexican out of the dark hole.

It was a very large panther of the blue type, and the Reynolds boys left at once with it for Fort Worth after they had carried it out on Geronimo's horse, to spend the Christmas holidays with the home-folks.

(Note: Geronimo was a very unusual Mexican in many ways; but his outstanding traits were his knowledge of wood-craft and his ability to walk on his hands; many times when we were driving cattle he would let some one lead his horse and he would toss his feet in the air and go walking along on his hands as easily as he walked on his feet. But like most athletes, he took pneumonia and died right now.)

A Mountain Quartette

A DRAMA IN THE WILDS

By WILL F. EVANS

From Sports Afield Magazine

No, they are not singers — unless you might call the night screams of the great cat of the forest, singing, as they give forth their weird challenge to other beasts that stalk forth by nightfall to pounce upon a luckless deer or calf.

The E V Ranch headquarters was founded in 1888 by George W. Evans; is located in a box canyon, and this canyon is a big nick cut out of a vast table-land of the Davis Mountains.

When you are on the table-land you can ride for 30 miles over great prairies and across canyons and foot hills and mountains, when suddenly you come to a great wall of rock, and as you gaze off below your eyes behold another country on another level 2,500 feet below where you are standing. Canyons ranging all the way from four hundred yards to ten miles in length break back into this table-land all around its western and northern sides, and in the days gone by these fortresses of the mountains have been the play-ground of the feline (panther) tribe which is fastly being de-populated.

On one memorable day our old pot lickers caused a big disturbance all morning up the canyon about a mile from the house; so four of we boys saddled up and went forth to investigate, being prepared for any emergency. Topping out the main canyon and going into Dead Man canyon we crossed a warm trail with the dogs we had with us; they immediately opened up in their wild tenor and bass, and the walls of the great chasm down which we were riding echoed the weird refrain, causing McAnelly to remark, "Gosh a'mighty! ain't they makin' the music!" and Joe answered back, "It's a panther, sure!"

After a hair-raising ride over the sleek rooks, leaping boulders and flirting with death around the edge of precipices, we caught up with the dogs on a very high point overlooking the main EV Canyon, but they were neither barking or doing anything else exciting when we got there; this did not discourage us however, as we had hunted panther before. So we dismounted and made our way off over the

(84)

rim, which was broken at this place enough so that we could climb down monkey fashion. All the while we were keeping a sharp lookout, for we knew the panther was perched out on some projecting pinnacle, or was back in some crevice, into which he had hidden when the closely pursuing dogs were making it too hot for him.

We were keyed to the highest expectancy, and every fellow was hoping that he would be the first man to get a shot. Presently McAnelly was the lucky fellow, for his gun went to his shoulder in Davy Crockett fashion and he put a 25-35 steel jacket bullet thru the head of a big panther, as the panther was in the act of leaping off and perhaps getting away, as it was in an inaccessable place and no dogs in sight.

Joe says, "There's another one around here somewhere. I can tell by the way the dogs are acting." So we went forth around under the main rim to hunt out some more hiding places. I was lucky this time, and I gazed up just in time to see a panther looking down at me from his perch 75 feet up directly over me. My next step would have taken me out of sight. There was only a part of his head showing, but I cut loose at that, and Joe yelled, "Jump! he's a coming!" — and my broad jump saved my life, as the beast fell right where I had been standing only a second before. He was not dead, but one eye had been shot out; and here he came with blood all over him, straight at us; but before we could fire, the crazed beast darted off into the brush down the mountainside out of sight. Presently he came into a little clearing, leaped upon a big rock and looked wildly about. He was a terrifying specimen, with his bloody one-eyed face, but I was quick enough and steady enough to put a 30 bullet thru him before he leapt again.

With our two trophies of the chase we came back into Deadman, and tho it was mid-afternoon and very hot, and the dogs were tired and sore-footed, still they wanted to start another trail; but we called them off and went home. After supper we saddled up and started out again into the inky black night, to see if there was still another panther up there in those breaks somewhere — for our dogs had caught the scent of another panther, which we felt sure was still in the canyon.

Just as soon as we reached the bottom of Deadman, the wild clarion notes of our mountain orchestra broke forth on the night air, and some one breathed the words, "Another one, by Jingo!" — and off we went, trusting entirely in the surefootedness of our ponies to save us from broken limbs or death. I am still living to tell about it.

After awhile the dogs ran the panther to bay on the highest pinnacle he could find, very sharp and narrow; so we tied our horses and made our way up to where the bedlam of yelping dogs and the angry growls of the panther were enacting a wild drama which made the pulse beat faster. We could not distinguish the dogs from the panther, as it was very dark, and we were afraid to get too close for fear the panther would jump off and get away; but we edged up close enough till we could lie flat down and skylight the whole panorama. We could see four dogs right on the rock with the panther, but he would make a pass at them and they would jump to safety off onto the next bench below, but others would take their places and they sure put up a pretty fight, altho an occasional deep-throated growl from the panther would send the cold chills creeping down our spines.

Joe worked his way up, amongst the dogs on the lower ledge, and as the panther lifted himself to strike at a dog the white hair on his neck and chest gleamed ever so slightly in the starlight, but it gave a second's target and Joe was quick enough on the trigger to put a bullet home. The panther leapt straight into the night and hit with a mighty thud 80 feet below in the narrow gorge of Upper Deadman Canyon, and all those dogs opened up their mighty chorus, and somehow or other, all the dogs and all the men were down there in less time than it takes to write about it, and we found the third panther the largest one of the lot — it was a monster panther — Joe had killed the biggest one. We were a proud and happy bunch as we rode into the ranch late that night — all except Lee, when he suddenly said, "Joe, I'll bet you anything that these panthers are the same bunch Mr. Weyer saw the other day headed for these mountains, and there were four of them. So there is still another one up there somewhere, and he belongs to me."

It was the only time in the history of our Western country that any one was ever known to see four grown panthers in one bunch, and when Mr. Weyer, who was operator of a station on the T. & P. Road, told my father that he had seen four together, my father did not believe it, and told Mr. Weyer that he must have had an extra bottle along, as panthers did not run in bunches.

However, at day-light, when the rest of us were dead to the world, Joe and Lee slipped out to the corral, saddled up and were gone with the sore-footed dogs to prove up the operator's story. A little while after breakfast — as we were skining ur panthers — our boys came riding in with another huge panther — Lee was right — and so had been Mr. Weyer.

(86)

Friend Jess Gets A "Bad One"

A BEAR HUNT IN THE RUGGED WILDS OF THE
WEST TEXAS CATTLE COUNTRY

By WILL F. EVANS

From Sports Afield Magazine

In a region little known to the outside world lies a strip of rugged country, forest-clad and perpendicular in most places, where for many years the black bear made his haunts and turned over the rocks hunting for bugs in lieu of something bigger to fill his paunch: and speaking of a bear hunting bugs; Uncle John Means was lolling on a mountainside one day absorbing a lot of the wild grandeur in the bear hunting country, leaving his horse to browse on the virgin grasses some distance away, when he heard a rock roll down the mountain nearby; looking up, he saw a large bear ambling along turning over the rocks with his paw looking for tid-bits to eat. The bear was completely pre-occupied, and was coming against the wind directly towards his observer, who wished to give Bruin a real shock. (The man had no gun with him).

When the bear got within a few feet of the silent watcher, this prankster commandeered his best bass voice to shout. "What're you doing there?" At which he saw only the flash of leathery heels in the split second of the bear's disappearance.

Jess Fisher's ranch lies in the very heart of these big mountains, and while his friends go speeding about in high-priced automobiles, Jess drove a pair of mules to a hack, or buggy, or four mules to a wagon when he went into FortDavis for goods. Or rode a horse over the wild range-land as he hunted cattle or followed his pack of hounds after bear or panther.

One day Frank Jones telephoned for Jess to meet him at the Kelly Ranch with his dogs as the bear had been catching his hogs; they met that night at the old ranch. By day-light a half dozen cow-punchers were mounting horses that were trying to buck them off; the dogs were un-leashed and they were on their way into the wilds of Goat Canyon, which is too rough and brushy for anything but goats and wild beasts. George Jones led them straight to where a bear had killed a hog the day before; and the dogs picked up a hot

Fightin
Black
Bear

Friend Jess Gets
a "Bad One".

Linda Faulk

bear trail at once. The rugged sides of Goat Canyon towered over head for hundreds of feet — the cliffs, the trees and the tumbled rock slides all were still hidden in that "darkest hour just before daylight".

As pre-arranged all the hunters except Jess headed for certain gaps in the high country to intercept the bear if and when he climbed out; Jess was to follow the dogs; and as the bear leads the dogs into and thru the roughest and most im-passable country he can find; and as the Kelly ranch horse was fat and soft, he could not climb out or leap the boulders like Jess's bear-hunting horses; and as the horse would not be lead over the bad places, Jess lost much time in finding a way out of the canyon.

The dogs had long since gone out of hearing; but when Jess got out on top he met Jones who had some of the dogs, and he said, "I heard a dog bark down in Pine Canyon awhile ago." Then about that time the rest of the pack took the trail. The men rode as far as they could go down the mountainside; then Jess divested himself of his pumper and his leggins, tied his horse to a tree and with his trusty rifle in hand scrambled off after the dogs.

The walls of Pine Canyon are rock-ribbed and nearly 4,000 feet high. The dogs were baying lustily down in the Canyon, and Jess was praying that he could get to the tree before the bear jumped out; but before he could reach the tree he could hear them on the run again; then came the real work when he followed in their wake up the opposite side of the canyon. Presently he heard shots out on top, and looking up, could see young Merritt Finley shooting across Pine Canyon with a high-powered rifle at the bear that was nearly a mile away to the east.

When Jess finally reached the top he was drenched in perspiration; but he forgot his fatigue when he heard the dogs at bay again on the east side of Merrill Canyon. He lost no time in getting down close to where the dogs were, but he had to circle around the head of a short canyon, and there were the dogs in a circle around a big black bear; he was at the base of a pine tree and the brush and grass was all beaten down where the dogs and bear had been milling around. About this time the enraged bear made a pass at a dog with his ears backed like a fighting horse; Jess saw it either had to be a dead bear or a dead dog, so he planted a bullet in the bear's neck; this checked the bear, but did not fell him. The bear now wheeled to fight off the dogs that were trying to ham him; he just knocked them right and left; then fell off into the gully out of sight, all of the dogs in hot pursuit. As he came up on the opposite side Jess poured a load into him behind the shoulder, and some of the dogs ran in and hammed him; then he wheeled with his mouth open and grabbed one and slapped two more over into the gully, and plunged for the brush again; but another well-placed bullet brought him over backwards down the hill. He was a dead bear now, and would kill no more hogs, or bite any more dogs.

After much horn blowing Jess finally got some of the boys in to the scene and dispatched one of them to bring his horse down into the canyon; and the fighting bear was carried out.

Desert scenery
(YUCCA)

Linda Faulk

A Record Trip In A Tin Lizzie

A COLD, WILD, CROSS-COUNTRY RIDE BEFORE THE ADVENT OF PAVED ROADS

By WILL F. EVANS

From Sports Afield Magazine

A few years ago, before the high-powered, high-priced cars came into practical usage by the ranch-men, they thought a Ford was the only car with which to cross the country in a hurry.

Means and Evans have ranches in New Mexico as well as in the Davis Mountains and the Pecos country of West Texas; and as two of the boys were going up to the H-Y Ranch managed by my brother Joe, I decided I would go along for the ride.

Our jitney was topless and doorless, and the fenders were tied up with baling-wire; and the noise it made was terrific; and the vibration something fierce.

At the un-seemly hour of 2:30 A. M., our little car left the Circle, one of the branch ranches of the Company, and headed out over the old wagon-road thru the sand towards Van Horn; and tho we were muffled to the eyes, the biting cold pierced us to the marrow in our bones. As we filled up with gas at the ranch, and had a supply of oil along, we passed thru the little towns of Van Horn, Sierra Blanca and Finlay without stopping; the night still enveloped us, while the poor lights of the old Model T made the negotiation of the sandy, crooked road extremely perilous; the wide, sand-filled draws posed a problem at each crossing, and usually two of us had to push while the driver steered across, giving the old car all it would take in low gear. (Today as the public glides along at 80 miles an hour over the smooth ribbon and speeds across the many concrete bridges, they little dream of the difficult hazzards of the pioneer drivers).

It began to get colder and colder, at this darkest hour just before day-light; and sometimes we would have to get out and run up and down the road to ward off the numbness from the cold.

Just at the break of day we reached the pavement at Fabens; and tho we felt the immense relief of traveling on cement after bucking the sand and the bumps so long, the cold became more intense; and from a recent rain which left puddles and lakes along the way, these were all frozen over to emphasize the fact that we really were having zero weather — only a heavy saddle-blanket in front of the radiator kept the water from freezing in our engine regardless of how hot the motor might seem.

We were in El Paso, enjoying a warm meal at an early restaurant by sun-up; we filled up with gas at Longwell's, and were again under way — out over the highlands in Sunset Heights, on by the Smelter with its massive smoke stacks; on by the Cement Plant, skirting close along on the banks of the Rio Grande, and enjoying the few remaining miles of the pavement which we struck at Fabens.

A few miles along on the old Mesilla road, and we turned sharp to the left, crossing the river at Mesilla Dam; then we topped out into the sand hills which lasted nearly all the way to Deming, and some of the sand was so very heavy that two of us had to push the car in many places; but a few miles out from Deming we struck the hard-surfaced ridges which lasted all the way to Silver City. As we negotiate this crooked roadway over a road smooth and hard, the giant Black Mountain Range appears to our right and the heavily timbered Burro Mountains to our left. The Burro Mountains are a paradise for goats and burros.

A sudden turn and we slide off into the picturesque little town of Silver, with its side-walks, paved streets and the general aspect of a real live city. Here we had a fine meal filled up our car with gas, and went climbing out from the Silver City basin, on the last lap of our trip, headed for the ranch 52 miles away. The road winds about over the hills, across the canyons, and along the "back-bones", with massive mountain ranges to the left, and the lofty Mogollons to the right, clothed with forests of pine, pinon, cedars and oaks, and rimmed with perpendicular walls of granite.

On across the famed Gila river, with many corn fields and frijole patches in this fertile valley, grown principally by Mexicans with their little herds of goats, a few cows and ponies; who have probably lived along this stream for centuries; then on up Duck Creek, a tributary of the Gila, where there are still more farms and ranches. Dusk gathered about us, and soon we were enshrouded with darkness, with the stars glimmering overhead in a brilliancy seen only in the clear atmosphere in the mountainous regions. The invigorating air swept into our lungs as we sped along the hard road in the H-Y pasture; and at 8 P. M., just 17 hours since we left the Circles, we had covered 360 miles. (In that day of bad roads and inferior cars, that really was a record — today, a driver could make it in 5 hours with high-speed car, and think nothing about it).

We enjoyed all the hospitality of the ranch for a few days then headed for Duncan, Arizona, via Silver City and Lordsburg — Duncan is the shipping point from the H-Y Blue Creek Ranch, where the boys were to ship out a herd of steers.

As the herd was crossing the Gila at Duncan late that evening, many of the cattle got stuck in the treacherous quick-sands, where they had to remain till the boys penned the others before they could go back into the cold water to dig the un-fortunate cattle out; they worked all night in the icy water by lantern-light; they got them all out but a few that drowned.

After helping the boys ship out, we left Joe with his outfit of cowboys, and about dark that night we headed east towards El Paso. But the cold was so very intense that we were numb by the time we reached Lordsburg. There were no modern hotels at this little mining and cowboy town, and what hotels were there were jammed with the travelers seeking shelter from the cold; but Huling found a friend who let us have a room for the night.

(Note: Today fine hotels and modern Tourists Courts grace the town of Lordsburg, with ample accommodations for the heavy traffic which passes over Highway 80.)

"Bear Trails"

A BEAR HUNT IN ONE OF THE WILDEST REGIONS OF THE DAVIS MOUNTAINS

By WILL F. EVANS

From Hunter-Trader-Trapper

I can see the twinkle of the camp fire, and feel the breeze as it fanned my cheeks as we rode off down the rugged point into the head of Nation's Canyon, one of the most in-accessible canyons in the entire Davis Mountains range.

As we crossed the divide between Madera and Nation's Canyons the sun was falling over the western wall of mountains, and with the setting sun, sprang up the evening breeze redolent with the essence of mountain verdure, as pure as the ozone itself.

Means and Evans joined "packs" with the Sproul's, the great bear hunters of the Fort Davis region; and they beat us into the the canyon — chaining up a couple of dozen dogs and staking out a dozen horses in the heart of the boulder-strewn jungle with the stars looking on, gives a jest to a man's appetite. Antelope steaks fried in bacon grease, cold biscuits, tea-cakes, hot coffee and pure mountain water — an exchange of jokes and bear hunting experiences around the bonfire of pine knots — then we crawl in between the blankets.

Out in the fastness of the mountains, "far from the maddening crowd", man can commune with nature and renew the well-being of his soul and his kinship with the Great Builder of the universe.

The jingle of tin-cups, frying pan and coffee-pot on the swinging back of a pack-horse, makes sweeter music to the old hunter than any other except the baying of a pack of "pot-lickers."

While it was yet dark, and it seemed as if we had just slipped our boots under the tarp, some early "bird" stirred up the coals and put the coffee on. We were soon all out and blinking around the fire, changing sides with the blaze and the crisp morning air which cuts very keenly when it is laden with frost.

Before the first faint light pales the east we are in the saddle, trying to keep all the dogs except Brownie, behind us; for these eager young dogs would be off after any kind of varmint which had left a scent on the ground the night before; while Brownie only opened up when a bear had been along.

The red-oaks, haw-thickets, tangled mustang-grape vines and piled-up boulders, with walls rising straight up on each side for hundreds of feet, makes bear hunting no pink tea-party affair; while many there be who hear the first refrain of the pack after Brownie sounds his "bugle"; but few there be, who reach the tree and take a crack at Bruin.

Just as it was getting light enough to distinguish each other from the myriad of shadows, Brownie sounded the alarm to "go over the top"; and going over the top from the depths of Nation's canyon is wind-breaking for both horse and man, as there are only a few places where a horse can top out at all, and many places the going is so terrible that the man has to dismount and climb out ahead of his horse.

The bear takes every advantage of gravity — he never attempts the vertical ascent of a mountain, but uses the tactics of the skilled engineer — he gets the grade, and his born instinct keeps him true on his course — when he finally tops out of a deep canyon he may be several miles from where he left bottom, and usually a long ways ahead of dogs and men. But he leaves out engineering then and only uses gravity when he literally falls off into the next canyon — he can beat a two ton rock to the bottom — then he can take his time in selecting his path up the next mountainside, but always picking a course where a man nor a horse cannot follow, and almost too rough for a dog.

On top, the packs split up and finally they all went out of hearing — the boys split up into squads and rode like the devil heading for famous gaps thru which a bear might pass, and for projecting points under which the fleeing bear might pass; and then you must shoot, and shoot to kill. To ride out onto one of these cliff-bound points, dis-mount and creep to the extreme brink and peer off into the depts below, makes the blood run faster. The stillness is almost over-powering, and the silence is so loud that it can be heard with ears attuned to the super natural — when this happens to you you are with nature in its eternal infinity.

I had a feeling in my breast that this particular point upon which I was crouched, was the place of enchantment; but the two other boys who had been breaking down the brush in heading for this same point, finally got the fidgets and decided to go on back to camp, and wanted me to go along, but the "still small voice" whispered to me, "Don't go yet awhile." And then — my heart almost jumped into my mouth, for a beautiful black bear pushed his way out thru a thicket and started shambling across an open space on a little bench a hundred yards below.

My gun flew to my shoulder, and again the still little voice whispered, "Draw low, draw low." I took the hint and drew a bead on him underneath his brisket — he fell with a bullet thru his heart, a black-robed beauty.

The other boys stopped at the crack of my rifle, which sounded like a cannon in the terrific silence; they rushed down to my side pumping a cartridge as they asked in hushed whispers, "Where is he, where is he? But the bear was a dead one when we got down to where he lay. His fur was soft, and black and extremely beautiful.

Only a few of the dogs came out on the trail, and they had gotten "balled" up in the roughs, so the bear would have gotten entirely away if my bullet had not ended his flight; as he was a long ways ahead of the dogs. I was very proud of my bear, but the other boys were sick at heart because they weren't the lucky ones. They rode out onto many points, dismounted and got out on the brink some distance away from their heaving mounts, and stood in strained attention, listening for the dogs which failed to come out — but they listened in vain.

We reached camp late with my bear — all the hunters were in but Mack Sproul, but as his entire pack was gone, we felt that he had gotten after a "running" bear and was still riding to try to call off his dogs. When a man turns his horse "wide loose" and risks his neck in trying to keep in hearing of the dogs when they are after a bear, and it is all over with, and he is back safe in camp, he can conjure up many things that can and might have happened to the fellow who has not yet reached camp by night-fall — so when Mack rode into camp late that night with a monster bear's foot tied on his saddle, we had a "war" dance around the camp fire, out of pure thankfulness.

Old Man Grizzly Puts Up Fierce But Futile Fight

SLAIN IN BLACK RANGE AFTER LONG EIGHT DAY CHASE BY EVANS BROTHERS, BUD McGAHEY AND L. INMAN

By G. W. (DUB) EVANS

In El Paso Times, Sunday, May 4, 1930

From out of the Black Range of the Rocky Mountains in south central New Mexico, about 175 miles northwest of El Paso and 50 miles northeast of Silver City, comes an unusual story of an unusual bear hunt which ended with the killing of a monster grizzly bear — a genuine grizzly weighing more than 1000 pounds — which had been foraging on stock of that region for more than 15 years.

The story as written by G. W. Evans, of Albuquerque, N. M., who was accompanied on the eight-day hunt by his brother Lee, Bud McGahey of Borger, Texas, and L. Inman, of the Healy ranch in the Black Mountain country, will be broadcast over WDAH at 7:45 o'clock tomorrow evening by Joe Evans, a brother of the two hunters.

For more than 40 years, the Evans brothers have been hunting bear in the Davis Mountains, Black and Mogollon mountain regions and this grizzly is the second they have ever killed.

The thrills of hunting the grizzly, according to G. W. Evans' story, by far eclipse all other kind of hunts.

OTHER BEAR TOO SMALL

In the story, Evans tells of another bear killed, but it was so small when compared with the big kill that little space is devoted to it. In commenting on the hunt last night, Joe Evans, who makes his home in El Paso, said the big grizzly had been the object of many hunts but had always been successful in eluding his enemies. Gov. Dan Moody, of Texas, an ardent bear hunter, had been considering returning to El Paso soon and accompany Joe Evans on a hunt for the killer of hundreds of cattle and sheep, but the hunt that started April 20 and ended April 28 with the killing of the big bear eliminated that hunt.

(But let G. W. Evans tell the story — Ed.)

(97)

SHORT BROWNIE KNOWS STUFF

"We moved from the ranch to the head of Black Canyon, taking two days to make the trip. We left the dogs tied up the first day, only taking Short Brownie to look for signs. We found a grizzly track about six miles from camp on the east side of the range. The track headed north. I took the dogs the next day and was to go down into the rough country where we saw this track. The other men took stands out on top at places where they thought the bear would come out if we got a start. The track we found the day before seemed to be old, but the dogs finally took it. They trailed it into a rough canyon about one half of a mile north and hit a red-hot trail. I had about 20 dogs, the most of them were young and had not been hunted with lately. They were fresh and anxious to run anything. Just as they went off under the first rim of this rough canyon, they hit the fresh trail of the bear where he came from a cow that he had killed about a half mile down the canyon just east of where I was. All the dogs except Little Brownie and one other dog took the back end of the trail that led down to the kill. I ran out to the edge of the bluff to listen and heard Brownie and this other dog barking — bayed right down under me. They had already come up on the bear and were not 100 yards from me. The brush was so thick I could not see the bear at all. I waited there a few minutes and could hear the bear breaking the brush as he walked around with the dogs barking at him.

LOT OF BLUFF

"There were a lot of bluffs there just over the bear and it sounded to me as though he was coming up the hill and was going to pass in west of me. I moved a few hundred yards west and when I got where I could listen, the bear had run east and right under where I had moved from. All the dogs that had gone on the back trail were out of hearing. I found out later that after they had reached the kill, they had scattered and were running deer and coyotes.

The last time I heard Little Brownie, he was still baying the bear and going southeast and just exactly away from where the men were stationed. They never did know what happened. It was too rough to ride so I followed Brownie on foot and could see this big old bear track ever once in a while. I finally lost the track and the wind came up, so I lost out entirely.

'I hunted for Brownie all afternoon. I went back to my horse at 12 o'clock and made a big circle but did not find anything. Dogs began to come to me, but no Brownie. I went back to camp late that evening, having most of the dogs. Little Brownie came in that night about 10 o'clock.

"While in the canyon where the cow was killed, I saw the track of another bear — a fair sized little bear. Three of Lee's dogs didn't come in so Lee and Inman went to the Ladder ranch to look for them and the rest of us moved camp. We moved about five miles south and camped in the saddle between the head of the Mimbres and Palomas creeks right on top of the Continental Divide. We had a pretty camp and a good place for our horses."

REVISIT KILL SCENE

"The next day, we all decided to go down near the kill. I was to take Little Brownie and go down to the cow and get the trail straightened out. Lee and Inman found Lee's dogs at the Ladder ranch and got back to our new camp late that evening. When I got down near the kill Brownie struck a trail and I soon found out that it was the little bear instead of the grizzly. The grizzly hadn't come back. Lee and Inman let the other dogs go when they heard Brownie, but it was a big, rough country and before the dogs could get to him he had gone into a rough canyon behind a point and neither the men nor the dogs could hear him.

"McGahey and Deming Inman had taken a stand at the head of the canyon that Brownie was going up. Most of the dogs that Lee and Inman had released had run off after a deer and were scattered all over the country, most of them going in the opposite direction to the bear. The bear came out in sight of Bud and Deming and they shot at him about 15 times. We all got together about where the shotting happened and saw Little Brownie go out where the bear had gone, by himself. We just waited where we were to put other dogs on the trail as soon as they come back to us. Inman and I waited there to gather up the dogs and the other boys went on out on top to work around to some deep "saddles" on top of the Divide in the direction the bear was going. Inman and I waited there about an hour and finally gathered up 11 dogs. We had to rim around the head of a rough canyon to get to the bear's trail. As soon as we got over there the dogs hit the trail and left in "high". We followed them but they crossed a rough canyon or two and left us far behind. We went on in their direction though, and found them treed in about the third canyon and only about one mile east of our camp. We killed this bear, a brown he bear, and as Lee and the other boys were in hearing distance, we all soon got together. I guess Little Brownie already had the bear treed before the other dogs got there, or he would have been much further off after having been shot at so many times.

BROWNIE STRIKES TRAIL

"The next morning we started south from camp and hadn't gone a mile until Brownie struck a trail and we saw that it was old big grizzly, going south right down the Government trail. He went right down the trail for about six miles and all of the dogs trailed him good. It was all we could do to stay in hearing, loping nearly all the time. They finally turned off east and followed near the main Divide for about two miles. They went off into the head of a very rough canyon and we heard them come up on the bear; these grizzlies don't run when the dogs come up on them. All six of us were together on this rough point and decided that Bud and I would go on foot as it was too rough to ride, and see if we could get a shot at the bear. There were eight or ten dogs down there and making a lot of noise. The brush was so thick one could only see a few yards ahead. The bear didn't stay there very long. I think we got within 50 or 100 yards of him before he ran. As soon as he ran, and the dogs overtook him again, he must have turned on them for they came back in a bunch to me. I think they all came back but Brownie and possibly one or two others. I hurried to the edge of a big point that they had gone over and when I got where I could look out, I heard Brownie off o n a mountainside, and locating him, saw him and the big bear going around the side of the mountain. Brownie was only a few feet from the bear's heels, and the bear was in a lope. There was one other dog behind Brownie, a black dog, but I don't know which one it was. It was either a dog of the Inman's, called Dobie, or Lee's Black Alice. The bear was headed south or southeast and going off into the north fork of the Animas.

SEPARATED IN CANYON

"It had begun to get pretty hot so I thought the bear might stop when he crossed the canyon as there were lots of big bluffs there, thick brush and a running stream of water. I hurried off the mountain, thinking sure I would get to shoot the bear as he crossed the canyon. Bud and I had gotten separated in the first canyon the dogs had crossed, where they had bayed the bear the first time. There were some big falls in the canyon and as Brownie was the only dog barking I soon lost hearing of him when I got near the water. There were 11 dogs with me at this time and none of them trying to follow the bear. I had lost hearing of Brownie and I did not know what had become of him except that I knew he had either quit or crossed the canyon. As he didn't show up, I figured he was still with the bear, so I sized up the country and picked out a saddle on the south side of the canyon that would be a likely place for the bear to come out. I climbed up to this saddle and found where the old bear had gone through with the dog tracks right in his. The other dogs took up the trail there and followed it. It began to turn west and into a still rougher country. As soon as I got well over onto the rim of the next canyon I could hear Brownie baying about a mile west of me. A few of the dogs went to him, but most of them came back. I could not get to him without crossing a country where I was satisfied the bear could hear me, so I decided I would go off into the canyon and up it to a point where I could climb out behind and come up on the bear from the opposite side. It took me about an hour to do this, and when I came up over the point where I thought the bear was, he had moved, but I was within about a hundred yards of him.

BRUSH AWFULLY THICK

"Several of the dogs went over to where he was but didn't stay long. The brush was so thick I simply could not see the bear though I was close enough and could tell where he was by the dogs. He kept moving and would only stay in one place a few minutes. This was about 12 o'clock and getting awfully hot. I kept climbing around after the dogs and the bear, and as I was so close to them, the dogs with me woud go to the bear every once and awhile, but would not stay long. The wind began to blow, and there were several minutes that I could not hear any dogs at all. I kept hunting around and could see the old bear's tracks. I knew he was giving out or too hot to travel, and he seemed to be determined not to leave this mountain he was on. It was about the roughest place in the country, and the brush so thick that a man could hardly crowd through it. I sat down on a rock at the edge of a point to rest, and had been there only a few minutes when I heard the dogs just below me, so I moved over a little further and could hear them plainly, only about two or three hundred yards right under me. I got down a few minutes later as it was all down hill. There were three dogs with the bear at this time — Black Alice, Dobie and Little Brownie. As I came near them some of the dogs went to them and began barking at the bear.

"I slipped down towards them and kept getting closser. I could only see for a few feet on account of the thick brush, but finally located the bear by the dogs. He was lying down with his right side to me. I could see his head moving up and down as he was panting. I was about 15 or 20 feet from him. I shot at about where I thought his shoulder was, or a little behind. He made an awful noise and began to beat the brush and bellowed like a bull. I got a little closer and could see he was staggering badly. I shot him again in the neck and he died in a few seconds. He was on a steep hillside but the brush was so thick he only rolled about 30 feet, breaking the brush as he rolled over it. I looked at my watch and it was two minutes after One o'clock. Not a dog bit him, even after he was dead. I never saw such a bear as he was. I caught hold of a foot and could not turn him over. I knew that if I did not get help the hide would be wasted, so I left the bear and went to a high point and shot three times. I sure was tickled when Lee answered me. He was within 300 yards of the bear when I shot him, and saw me on the point as I gave the three signal shots. We began to talk to each other and decided what to do about getting the hide out.

"We decided to get his horse as close as to the bear as we could and skin the bear, then bring the skin out on Lee's horse. We got back to the bear at three o'clock and got him skinned by five. We got the skin back to the horse and then worked our way off into the canyon by dark where there was water, and there we stayed till morning. Then we loaded the skin and began to climb out toward the top of the mountain where we had left the boys and horses the day before. Lee walked and led his horse all the way out; and the huge skin was so heavy that the horse gave out carrying the load. But if it had not been for Lee's horse being near the scene of the kill we never could have gotten the skin out at all.

"We got out on top about 10 o'clock and met the boys with some food and fresh horses. We got the skin to camp about three o'clock. When we went the next day to get some pictures of the bear's carcass, we found that there was another Grizzly on the same mountainside where the boys first came upon the bear, and found where the other bear had gone out. We decided that as our horses were pretty well tired out and our grain supply running low, we would pack up and move out toward home instead of sending for grain to continue the hunt.

"The little Bear were getting so thick that we could not go in any direction without striking a trail. When we moved out of camp we led Little Brownie to keep him off bear trails. He struck trail even with a collar and chain on.

The wild turkeys were plentiful and we could hear them gobbling from early morning until latte in the evening."

Rounding-Up On The Slash Ranch

IN THE WILDS OF THE BLACK MOUNTAINS AND THE ROUGHS ALONG THE GILA

By WILL F. EVANS

From K. Lamity's Harpoon

SLASH HEAD-QUARTERS AT BEAVERHEAD

The sun had already dipped over the western wall of mountains as we climbed the steep grade above the old lake; topping the rise, we got our first view of the Vega and got its pungent smell of eve-ning-time; then the great ranch house broke into view as it snuggled against the rocks in the glen. The appetizing aroma of roast-beef, frijoles and "Son-of-a-gun" ticked the nostrils of we travelers from the Davis Mountains.

At this time, in the year 1920, Joe M. Evans was General Man-ager of the Evans Bros. New Mexico ranch, and Dub Evans was Foreman. (Dub soon became manager as well as foreman).

There was a great re-union as we gathered around the chuck-box that eventful night; and plans were being made for the annual Summer work, to brand up the big calves and gather fat stuff to place in the holding pastures till time for market. These fat cattle had to be driven 80 miles to the shipping point. (The big cattle-trucks were not then in operation).

The night air is really invigorating in the Black Mountains, as the creek-beds are 6300 feet above sea-level; the table-lands 7500 and the peaks 9300 feet. Pure mountain air and pure mountain water made one's very existence extremely delightful.

By day-light we were all up and stirring about, loading on beds and camp equippage; and by sun-up the four-mule chuck-wagon was climbing out of the canyon, with the cook, Lee Williams handling the reins.

The mules were fat and frisky, and broke the tongue out of the chuck-wagon the first steep gully Lee attempted to cross; so when our calvacade reached the scene, the four mules, the wagon-tongue and the cook were all tangled up in the same harness.

We patched up the wreckage and moved on over the wild moun-

Noon Meal at Doney Lank

tain road; Paul and his wife and three small children were in one buck-board; Joe and his wife and Dub's wife and our mother were in another buck-board with two of the babies: the writer drove a four-mule wagon loaded to the bows with beds, and etc., with his wife and small daughter and Lee's two small daughters.

Dub and some of his cow-boys drove the horses; we had brought along five saddles from Texas; these were placed on horses which were driven along with the remuda.

Along about noon, as I reached the brink of a mountain, and looked off into a canyon which made my head swim, I un-loaded my wife and the children and sent them on down the zig-zag road-way ahead of me; about a third of the way down I met my wife coming back, white and terror-stricken; she had come upon the wreck of Joe's buck-board, now lying off down the hill with its wheels in the air. (This was a flimsy affair; and the team of mules were as wild as jack-rabbits).

We breathed a great sigh of thankful relief, when we found the occupants all safe and sound at the foot of the hill. But my troubles really began then. Mace and Beulah rode two of the horses, and Joe rode on horse-back also; but I had to haul all of the kids; mother rode with Paul.

It was long past the lunch hour when we reached the great divide; but Lee soon had us a real meal with plenty of coffee.

Out under a towering pine tree over-looking Toony Tanks the magnificent view of the broken terrain with the lofty Mogollons (Mo-go-yones) in the blue distance, was awe-inspiring.

Our road became ever more rugged as we began to make the descent into the Gila Canyon region. At last we reached bottom where the log-cabins of Horse Camp gave promise of shelter and of the good ranch-chuck which has made ranch-life famous.

The tall form of J. B. Derring, in charge of the Horse Camp ranch, emerged from one of the door-ways with a warm handclasp and a word of welcome to all. It really gets lonely down in these wilds, a long ways from no-where; and a cow-boy who has been batching all winter and spring, is really over-joyed to have human companionship at any time.

All around about, the pines rise in majestic splendor; a mile down the canyon the cliffs tower upwards for hundreds of feet, getting more jagged and spectacular as they approach the Middle Fork of the Gila (Heely) River.

The first day out, we worked the horse and bull pasture, the south side of which is walled in by the bluffs of the Middle Fork; the next day we topped out around to the south-east; off into East-water spring canyon; then on out to Green Fly tank at the south base of the Black Mountains; on one side is steep mountains, black with timber; on the other, long open ridges reach all the way to Gila.

I went with Dub and my father to make a drive up in the brush and in a very short time after Dub had sent me off to hunt a short canyon out I jumped a bunch of old out-law cattle which had been getting away for years. The black, streak-faced pony, really became electrified; and I crowded those fleeing cattle so fast that I turned them before they reached their favorite get-away-gap, and forced them to take to the long mesa which was rim-rocked entirely around the point. They had gone into a regular mountain-trap; and the next day Dub, Paul, Graves and J. B. went back and tied all five of the out-laws down; then drove a bunch of gentle cattle to the spot, and brought all the wild ones in to the ranch with them.

There is a large spring of pure mountain water which breaks forth a short distance from the Horse Camp cabins; and this water is really nectar for the gods.

After a few days in camp, Lee and Lou C., came across the mountains from head-quarters, bringing a pack-horse laden with goodies from Magdalena for the kiddies: there were 9 children under 9 years old, and three more under 12; an even dozen kids; and it took a lot of fruits and confections for this bunch.

New Mexico cowboys have long square boxes, raw-hide covered, with rope handles, that they hook over the pack-saddle horns; they fill these boxes up with every thing imaginable, cover the whole job up with water-proof tarps; strap it on with a diamond-hitch; and it is impossible for the pack-animal to either pitch it off or drag it off in the low-hanging brush. In Evans Bros. pasture there is much game of all kinds, but they are well protected by the Forest Rangers, who also serve as Game Wardens; these employees of Uncle Sam, also guard the pine trees, and an axe is never put to one without a permit. It is a noble deed to preserve a tree which nature has been so long in the growing.

The average height of the pine trees in the Black Mountains is a little better than 80 feet, but many of them are 120 feet high; they are almost devoid of knots for 40 or 50 feet from the ground; the bark is straight and yellow.

Our whole calvacade, with the addition of a herd of cattle, trek back to the ranch at Beaverhead; we have a couple of big round-ups at the Lake; then head south for the lower ranch on the Gila. For four miles the going is good; but we soon quit the Beaver and climb out over the mountains and across the canyons, till finally we work our way off down a long, rough road into Taylor Canyon. The peaceful scene repays us for the many hard jolts we took in getting there; a clear stream of water flows softly over the smooth pebbles; while the water-cress bobbles with the ripples, and the waters are frescoed with the shadows of the cotton-woods over-head. Here we noon at this delightful spot in the canyon.

Then we splash along down the stream and watch the minnows dart from under the wagon-wheels; we are walled in with cliffs of many colors; the wild-grape vines entwine themselves about the face of the cliffs; the black walnut trees with their wonderful foliage are scattered along the way, and also many trees and under-brush of a water growth. Soon we meet up with the Beaver, a stream larger and more beautiful than the Taylor; these two streams form the Gila River. Now we have some real water to cross and follow down; the willows are so rank that in many places they choke up the road-way; we are in a maze of under-growth almost too dense to negotiate.

Soon the old log cabin on the point comes into view; here we shake hands with Sim Smith, the Boss of the Gila, and his fair help-mate, who roams the hills with Sim and rides like a real cow-boy. Sim is a type seldom seen; long, lank and hungry looking; utterly fearless; as ugly as a picked turkey, but a heart of gold beats beneath that ugly exterior.

The rains settled in on us, and after a few days camped out in the wet, we were glad to get back to head-quarters; taking a short cut up Undertaker's Hill. (It was entirely too steep and dangerous to negotiate on our way down).

HOMEWARD BOUND

The fog was lifting from the Vega; the low-sailing clouds were dragging their mist on the canyon walls as our cars coughed along over the mountains around the lake. The way was wet and soon got wetter as the heavens began to darken; we plowed thru mud and a sheet of falling water for 35 miles; we were tired and hungry, and finally made a fire out of water-soaked wood; boiled some coffee and broiled some bacon. The clouds lifted while we enjoyed our meal; but the rains set in again in torrents.

Our cars bogged down one after the other; and as fast as we pulled and pried one out, another would go under.

We fought them till night-fall trying to reach the Benton Ranch up the main draw; but we had to "lay out" all night, sleeping as best we could in the cars, wrapped up in what bedding we had along.

Never did hot coffee, and a breakfast taste better, as we ate with the Benton boys at their ranch the next morning; and we rejoiced with them because of the bountiful rains.

The paved roads really felt good when we did finally reach them in the El Paso area.

FINAL CHAPTER

There will always be "Big Time" wherever a bunch of cowboys get together, whether around the chuck-wagon or in a hotel lobby; there will always be round-ups as long as there are cattle to round up; there will always be good horses as long as there are cowboys to train them.

And there will always be Rodeos as long as there are wild horses to handle and vicious bulls to ride and game cowboys to subdue them.

Also there will always be hunters for big game as longs as there is big game in the wild regions of the earth; and there will always be trained dogs to hunt with, and great hunters to follow the hounds.

The un-quenchable spirit of the old Pioneer beats strong in the breasts of the on-coming generations.

THE END.

INDEX